JAMES LIDDY

The Doctor's House

An Autobiography

salmonpublishing

Published in 2004 by Salmon Publishing,
Cliffs of Moher, County Clare, Ireland
web: www.salmonpoetry.com
email: info@salmonpoetry.com

ISBN 1 903392 39 X

A CIP record for this title is available from the British Library.

Cover Artwork: Author photographed with his father, Dr. James Liddy, at home
in Coolgreany, Co. Wexford, c1950
Cover Design & Typesetting: Siobhán Hutson

Salmon Publishing gratefully acknowledges the financial
assistance of The Arts Council/An Chomhairle Ealaoín

To dead colleagues:
Kay Boyle, Janet Dunleavy, Mel Friedman, Nic Kubly

To dead publicans:
Jack Cleary, George Fitzpatrick, John French, Christy Murray,
Kit Nash, Paddy O'Brien, Vincy O'Rafferty, Frank Olson,
Bill and John Scott

To comrades:
Jim, Liam, Tomás, Eric

Acknowledgements

Excerpts from this book have previously appeared in the following journals:

Blue Canary, Eire-Ireland, London Magazine, Metre, New Hibernia Review, Patrick Kavanagh Journal, Poetry New York, and *The Shop.*

1

The Doctor's House

If you had as good a time in the Adirondacks as I had in the County Wexford (the Yalla-Belly County) then you must have had a very good time indeed. For one month the sun shone day and night in the County Wexford....

—James Stephens

Angle-sloping barrack shed, big tree strung behind it, before it, big thick logs of wood. They've been saving them and piling them up. I'm afraid of the saw, it reminds me of the French Revolution. The old garden gates, fortress gates, one of them opened, the laurel hedge clipped quite low along the barrack wall. After mid-summer I don't go out there any more with the insects, red bites that are painful all night. I stay in the yard. The wood is piled up, it takes up a quarter of the space, someone has put a bicycle against the logs, a lady's bicycle. The black Ford is in the shed, it is usually out to patients or the golf club. Daddy must be in the Dispensary getting his things in the black bag together, making up the little bottles of medicines. Lots of cough bottles. They swear by it. The dogs run around: Ginger, Mi-Wadi; golden paws and ears, gold wag of tail in the month of July. Month of roses framing the doors and windows on the yard. Clematis gone now from the barrack wall on the drive, the stones in the wall are always loose. Lilac trees in the front, purple and white equally balanced, the red drops of fuchsia alongside. In the sheds, dead car batteries and pictures of dead jockeys and horses, the swallows make a mess when we leave the car in at night. I think of horses in here and their hay, that must have been a fine sight and a fine smell. Because there are no cars on the road, except the priest's and the doctor's, people travel by trap; with the logs, sometimes there's no place for the patients to park. The Condrons of Castletown come in the biggest and shiniest trap.

Our house is near the bottom of the village street, it's in a hollow, Wexford is full of hollows. You get the sun, but there's no view. A kind of trapped feeling. Mammy talks about Jordan's Hollow, by a bridge off the main road; Daddy visits there now to attend Liam Mellows's mother who is sick. Mammy says she thinks Daddy doesn't know who Mellows is; he has no politics. We had ghosts in the yard today, the wardrobe Mammy bought at Bauman's arrived in a big van. She says she is sure there are ghosts hiding in it; I hope they don't try to get out. The auction there was wonderful, a lovely white cream house, Mammy says it definitely dates from Queen Anne. Stables and rolling lawns and trees created by Protestant refugees from Bohemia. A man came up and showed us where a man had been hanged in 1798 on a spike on the gate of the yard. Strange noises never stop in the house, it's haunted a hundred times over. The last of them who just died, Miss Emily, is supposed to run up the avenue as a hare. Miss Lee, in Castletown Post Office, a patient of Daddy's, used to put Miss Emily's letters in a special bag and the postman delivered them before other mail.

Mammy keeps repeating that Daddy is a good doctor. She tells me he drinks tea with his patients; she drinks only Bewley's coffee. Every morning in bed, with maybe a poached egg and several cigarettes. He drinks tea in selected farmhouses—with the Symeses up in Wingfield, and with the Halpins in another hollow near the village. Nearby is Kinsellas of the Mill where he goes too for his cake; men in that family are still called Master, country people go there for the mill, it's very up-dated, it's just been electrified. Daddy is always on the road; he's gone for hours. With all these country lanes, I think sometimes of hiding away, I'd like to fly away, run away maybe, getting out of the hollows and all. I have the best and most beautiful times dreaming of this. When you put your mind to it, you can hear imaginary bells ring in the hedges and among the foxgloves. The friends you can't make around here are now yours. There is an end to imagining, though, because the Irish sing that at the furthest point of all roads the cemetery waits. That's where you escape to: the overgrown silence of the grass on the graves. Mammy never visits her mother's plot in Glasnevin, didn't even put up a headstone to her, I'm sure I will be the same when the time comes. All I'll want is the silence of the person that's gone, and I'll dream about that. That's walking the roads more than lovers, that's saying your prayers with your heart doing the walking. Mammy gets a Mass said for her mother every November, that's when Fr. Shine comes to afternoon tea. It's also afternoon coffee.

We are going for a swim today via Castletown. Croghan, gold-bearing mountain, the hamlets, tilt towards the sea. The narrow roads are full of potholes and small, sharp, stones. We cross the main road at Inch, not by the rambling house of the Rector, who comes to dinner with his wife, but by the gunner's cottage, (he was wounded in the Boer war), then past Hyde Park. The beaches are stoney some years, some years not. The little road winds at the sea's edge from Clone; a farmhouse or two. Down the lane through the open gate to Kilpatrick; park the car on the grass by the sandhills. Pull out the swimming togs and towels on the back seat, jump down on the sand, take off your shoes for the soft feeling, but mind the stones. The chimneys of the burnt-out Coast Guard Station prop over the highrise sand-hills at the end of the strand. There's a marsh, a silky pond with reeds, rushes; sometimes ducks. Over the wild flower hills and bunkers there's a different world, ocean flat as a bog with white crests; a ship or trawler far away. Say a prayer before water, you walk out quite a way before it gets deep, at the start, it's piled-up stones hurt your feet. You dip in or a wave comes, it freezes you for a long moment, you kick your feet, you plough your hands, you float looking up at the blue and white tent.

We used to go to a soft sandy beach at Clone; you climb down to it on a precarious path. We used to camp, have picnics, birthday parties, dig up the sand, have pieces of cake in the castle. Here I learned to swim. It's easy if you like waves; they punch you about and you float between wavelets with water in your mouth, and sometimes there's a heavy wind. Father held me; a good swimmer, he could swim for ever. Mammy only goes in on the hottest days without a puff of wind, she paws around doing the breast stroke for a few seconds. She says she prefers the lake temperature at Potsdam.

We spend forever and a day at the beach. I don't know how the time goes so fast—it's not Kilkee where you go for three or four short swims, at least before meals. Daddy says his mother made him swim before breakfast and he used to starve. There you're an Atlantic sprite or a mermaid, you could head off to New York, where Mammy comes from, in a second. You have the Pollock Holes, diving from boards or rocks, ladders down ledges at Myles Creek or New Found Out, but at Clone you have to rush into the water and when you're tired from getting cold you duck in. Only waves hitting you are interesting. Wales is over the horizon, not New York.

It's a fright when you find someone else on your beach territory. We didn't see the cars, but the Brennans were on our patch, and not just the Brennans; their friends the Beckers, the tea merchants from Dublin. He's German some way. Joe Becker has those blonde daughters undressing on the beach. Pat Brennan, bread king of Arklow, is in charge as usual; he's a dandy Mammy says. They're opening baskets and hampers, they're going to be in possession a long time. We get back in and wave from the car. We aren't always in Castletown just for a swim. There's winter, special occasions; Mass, where the men and women sit on opposite sides of the aisle. Families don't sit together, we do. The people there are Republicans, Daddy says they're suspicious of the church. They don't give anything in the collection box; Fr. Dunne talks about the buttons he finds there, very cross under the biretta. Now he's got cancer, Daddy says, and he finds it hard to amuse him. We always sit on the last bench, at the back.

One day we went to Castletown for the unveiling of Liam Mellowes's grave. It was pouring rain; that man was there—Mammy doesn't care for him. He was standing on a platform outside the cemetery wall, an umbrella held over his long trailing cloak. Small glasses perched on a big nose: the eyes going blind of the schoolteacher. The tall uncrowned king of Ireland in the national rain. Daddy could walk a mile up anyone's political bóthareen so Daddy was talking to him and asked me to come over to shake his hand. I got out of the car quickly and ran crying up the road towards the Presbytery. Mammy's son! Mammy's pride!

The front garden is a little paradise; walled, and divided in the middle by a path of white stones. As you descend the front steps, there is an inner sanctum of big blocky bushes, and on the other side a short drive into the back courtyard. The colours of the six bushes vary, I like the one with red and yellow blossoms, a sort of fuchsia with yellow bells as well as red hanging on it. On the street wall a lovely white bush parades. Daddy is talking about cutting down these shrubs, he's stupid, he wants to put in gravel so cars can be parked in the front, as if there isn't enough room in the yard. How can cars be as nice as leaves and blossoms? He's the same about the old hump-backed stone bridge on the lower street, narrow file with views of the stream on either side, furze and slowpoke water. He wants a wide concrete bridge to gleam.

Maybe there's something in doctors that doesn't understand. The doctor before Daddy (there were a few brief ones in between) was he the same 'improver?' At least Doctor Murphy chose the bushes and the white stones; he came by them recently, a tall haggard man in a large overcoat with an ancient Girl Guide wife. He strode up to the door, his door, past me, and banged the knocker. Inside to poor Mammy who couldn't offer them, or herself, a drink. I didn't hang around to hear what they were saying, he uses the word "bedad." His son died of an operation in Aden. Mrs. Kelly, who comes in to help the cook with the wash-up, says that Dr. Murphy's blood really gets up around the twelfth; he goes up to the North with his suit and bowler hat and sash. For a few days before he says things like, "If I don't get my dinner in a few minutes some Roman Catholic blood will be spilt around here." In the kitchen, I know it's hard to believe!

Doctor Murphy used to keep ducks in the back. Vincey next door says he'd clip one of their wings so they couldn't fly away. All the stories about him. Once on the hunt his horse bolted and he held on the saddle over the top of Annagh, a steep hill. Mammy says he's a horse Protestant, but everyone rode horses then. Lennon, the draper across the road, tells me he used to have a peculiar time with him. Doctor Murphy received the post first, but Lennon went to him and said things had changed: this was a new Ireland. The draper is a Fianna Fáil bottlewasher who comes to our house for election results; Dev wins, curse him. We and Mrs. Kelly in the top shop have a radio. People regarded the doctor as a god and Doctor Murphy had a cure, bread soda and water in a glass. Even Lennon takes it.

The tennis court out the back is lovely when Tom Bolger has worked on it; the white lines on the cut grass, and he has put up the net (Tom swears the usual tennis court oaths). The summer house, a kiosk, is under a bulky palm tree. It's thatched. We discovered treasure when we arrived: the croquet box with mallets, hoops, and balls. We put them up immediately on the court and played the game of the empire. Palm trees and croquet! Tennis parties. A table of drinks and jellies. White lines, white clothes, lager and white drinks in summer time. Being sent into the house for ice. Birds darting out of the hedges and getting nearly caught under the strawberry and raspberry nets; the windcharger on the way to the house, a little Eiffel tower. The laurels are getting very high at the other end, between us and the Byrne's orchard which is always getting robbed. Apple trees, cookers mainly, Doctor Murphy or Mrs. Murphy's trees, sentinels to the old order. Our pear trees down in the yard: the pears either disappear or end up on the ground. They never get to September to ripen, Mammy repeats each year.

Daddy doesn't see Doctor Murphy's crowd, they aren't his patients either, they usually go to Doctor Connolly in Gorey. I saw Colonel Grogan's funeral out the window, the gentry in the old carriages taken out for the war, faces with money in Lloyd's—a contrast with another procession going in the opposite direction, Mrs. Leonard's (who has a guitar) baby who died at birth; a small coffin in an ordinary hearse, people in everyday clothes behind, a big crowd with more waiting in Ballyfad. O'Rafferty's pull down the shutter on the roller when a cortege passes. Daddy looks after them, and the others too. He likes the Protestants, specially the ones not quite at the top. They pay and give you good tea and cakes. The Symeses are his favourites, Wingfield I think is the name of their place, it's near the Gap, he goes there on Thursdays. He must talk the price of cattle with them, and news of the empire. Lovely people, they will go to heaven with the Book of Common Prayer in their rosaryless hands.

The local Cromwellians are the Ellises; fancy land, sweet meadow by the river that goes under the bridge where you can see the village on its hill or look at Croghan over Lennon's field gone wild. The long meadow is the kind you see in an English print. Wood with narrow paths, bluebells. I go with Maggie who works in the Dispensary, we come on a small lake with a stone border, reeds and bamboos. You see high walls in the distance, Maggie says, that's the kitchen gardens. They have several gardeners working there all the time. The train passes noisily a few hedges away, you can only hear it faintly from the village, we sit talking about the families there, I try to remember which cottage is which name. I remind myself to keep Maggie in good humour, take my shoes off at the door so I won't muddy the floors she's polished. I always rush in and tell Mammy things. I see her now thinking of antiques or bridge or how she doesn't like the Liddys. Amused shining eyes. There's Freddie Cudlip the chauffeur pushing down the drive in the old Bentley. He winks under his cap.

The village street! The Pear Tallon used to live where Lennon's shop is. He was beaten up one day by the Ryans, a pagan family who lived with their cattle; they thought he was putting a thread across the street to their knocker. They would come out of their door with sticks. Old Reid, sitting in front of his orchard or his yellow yeoman house. He has a brother Bill, an R.I.C. man, they call him the most polished man in the village he dresses so "cleanly." He walks to the Church of Ireland at Inch every Sunday or saunters into O'Rafferty's for a drink, though behind his house are fields and bogs that belonged to the O'Raffertys. Emergency men! Up over that the green wooden facade of the Post Office, Birdie O'Rafferty, arms akimbo, huge black hat with hairpin, with her man Bernie Moran behind the counter. Bernie is not married, he is mad about women. He combs his hair and makes himself up when women drop by to post their letters.

Harvest is a god, it's a rural place. It was the greatest last year. We went to three threshings last year, one at Lennon's, one at the top of the Village, the other in Ballyfad. The machine makes so much noise, such piston shoving belt slithering and pushing. Many men in the sun cutting and stacking the field, "the steam." Nora and I helped carry the pails out to them, I think there was tea and milk in them. We got a ride home on a big stack of hay, floating on top, hayseed for ever in our clothes.

Daddy did a dangerous thing recently, Mammy tells me. He had to go up the hills to commit a man to mental hospital. He went with the guards in several cars up a long road to Langrell's. A brother of the man had killed someone at Inch a few years back. Isaac Langrell did the deed, he was in O'Brien's pub and in a dispute the two were put outside.

Langrell took a knife and cut the other man's head off right by the main road; they were watching it out the pub window. Luckily Daddy had no trouble. The postman also tells me about it, he never goes to that farm without being afraid of his life. One of the brothers, Willy, plays music all day, he has an accordion and melodeon and gramophone and wants you to go to his room to listen to his singing—he can't sing. Kelly the workman there churns the butter and throws it on the potatoes, then he knocks on the ceiling to bring them down. Another brother Dick got arrested at Hollyfort in his pony and trap with lovely rubber wheels; the guards were waiting for him. The local fellows had told Dick he didn't have to pay rates or taxes. There are no girls in the house. Isaac hated women, the other fellow Noblett, from Mayo, teased him about it. He had the knife in his hand and used it. Some of the fellows in the pub hid in the river.

Daddy says by the kitchen sink, "I'm only going to get six gallons a month." He read out the Department's letter:

priests, doctors, to get six gallons. August, the black market month, here we come. The car had to reside entirely within the Dispensary District; Mammy and I can't go under the leaves, big trees, to shop in Arklow or Gorey. Daddy is shopping under the counter up in Croghan. Anyway there is no fruit, Mammy talks about bananas, peaches. I barely remember the Frys bars with coloured centres. Mrs. Bond's store is for ration coupons; the top shop has a secret room of goods ordered before the war, more than drinking goes on. We get into the car after supper and glide as far as Arklow, coast in neutral, park on the back road, walk down to the Paramount or Ormond for Laurel and Hardy, The Three Stooges, The Bowery Boys. Rebecca breaks my heart, hardly a dry eye in the balcony. Mammy and Daddy are too old for the pictures; they go to Josie's hotel or the Golf Club. We meet, go up the blacked-out streets to the guilty car by the soaring lump of St. Saviour's; Mammy jokes about Winston Churchill's cousins, I am depressed by celluloid romance. I compose an imaginary dialogue, God: "Where did you find out about life before it started?" "In the Ormond Cinema of Jamesie Kavanagh, your honour." Daddy is fast behind the wheel home, he worries about tomorrow's meat from Redmond's, The Market House Gorey, to be picked up at Inch from the bus, a safe drive within the law.

We slip into town in the daylight when we can. Daddy goes to the hospital on Ferrybank, built by Billy Wicklow's father for his mother. I wander around. An Abbey cemetery behind the houses on Main Street, lower down past the winding shops the thatched Fishery, whitewash contrasting with women's black shawls, basins of fish for sale on the pavements, back yards of pickled herrings. Three-masters in the square harbour in front of the Pottery, two abandoned sinking schooners in the river; fishermen who have been all over the world, who may like other fisherman but don't relish Picasso, fishermen or deep sea sailors with pencil and sketch book in their heads, up rivers into lecherous cities: pints in either the lower or upper O'Raffertys. Wages of the sea, pints as dark as war, daily fist fight. Horse grazing on the old Mass grounds. Shawls, shawls, suddenly opening by the Pottery onto the beach, stones and waves, deserted, patches of beautiful washed pebbles, golfers some distance in. Mammy prefers the North beach with the crazy stakes, stout wooden poles like small blocks put up to protect the munitions factory against the Germans, blown up who knows how one day, a burnt out clock tower, a ruined Mayan city on the harbour. Mammy sits on the rug without a grain of sand, nothing encroaches on her sunbathing; she is a Riviera lady. She is back in Nice, she knows French, but Daddy has to speak to the gendarme for directions, to the waiter ordering sauced dishes Ghosts of Kynocks, a South African arms manufacturer behind us; trains full of workers coming from Enniscorthy, Rathdrum, Wicklow, Tinahealy; in the middle O'Rafferty's, Felix had a hundred pints waiting on the counter as the midday roar came over the bridge. Men in thirst, Mammy says!

This is a quiet spot on the beach at the Northern end, the nuns swim here and the aged Canon takes a dip some afternoons in a strange clerical costume, a sea horse in sea water. On a slope, above an array of bushes and trees, is the hospital Daddy goes to, The Countess of Wicklow Memorial Hospital! He is doing a call there now, the patients like him, they prefer him to Doctor Byrne, the nurses glow over him, their matron Miss Woolfe is his confidant. Mammy is a friend of Nurse McGrath's, one of Clare's Dragoons, they get drinks from Sally, a Victorian barmaid they call her, and sing at the end of the Golf Club night. When Daddy comes down he will complain about the old x-ray machine they have up there.

Above the hospital, Ballyrichard hill, called for Richard II, betrayed in Shakespeare and the inventor of the handkerchief. When the King lay in his tent on the hill, surrounded by hawthorns and heather, he was constantly attended by his hairdresser, that is why he got into trouble, Mammy tells; meanwhile, his soldiers were starving and when the provision ships stood off the sandbanks at Arklow the soldiers fell on the supplies, running over each other. Mammy points over to the Protestant spire, over there lies the ground of the King's enemy, the chieftain Art MacMurrough Kavanagh. So it's called Glenart, though now with gates, gatehouses on the Woodenbridge road with the Careysfort strawberry leaves, cottages with that coronet in Johnstown, Aughrim, Kilcarra, and through Arklow. On the Coolgreany road, there's another entrance and that passes Lamberton House, probably the dower house, where Mammy says the Rector fled in his nightshirt at the approach of the rebels in 1798. An oak drive to the yellow brick castle with its subdued massive tower burnt in our time (on a Sunday morning, people whisper, for their pride in building St. Saviour's that cathedral of a church); behind the mansion the hanging gardens. Mammy and I go there for vegetables and we wander around: terrace folds on terrace, each one crammed with workers holding shovels. We stand at the top at the turreted gate, we watch a disappearing cornucopia.

The hill, and the T.B. patients out in beds in the open, the sandhills over the sandcastles the Burma road from the town to the beach, the debris of factory buildings, the new Pottery on the other side of the river.

The cupola and the spire.

Spread around us. Look the other way, Mammy, Daddy, the ocean.

War

Franklin Roosevelt tells our government all about truth, justice, freedom, tyranny. The Irish don't listen, no soft touch. Churchhill lights his cigar, the Irish are worried by the cigarette ration. The sea hags flash the light off Kilmichael. Maybe there was more there than sea hags. We stand with the sergeant looking out the window of the grey room, moping about lights out at sea. Friends, foes, Germans? The sergeant with torch isn't worried, he wants to defend the neutrality of his country, he doesn't want to work too hard. "It could be an Irish boat, I'll go down there in the morning."

The war is somewhere else, it is hidden somewhere. It's in the car. It is time for the news. I like it so much I threatened to smash the car window the other day if they didn't let me in to hear it. We drive off, I'm behind the two adults who don't often talk too much, today there's a discussion, "The Germans seem to be caught in Stalingrad." "They'll be able to get out." "You think Hitler is making the same mistake as Napoleon?" "There's an awful lot of snow in Russia."

Mammy has a scotch, she's talkative about the war. She gets on to our wars, "Your father's people were different, worrying about law and order, they burnt letters the time the British were searching Limerick, they don't sign their telegrams. My mother's people were for the cause. In 1917 we gave our car to de Valera, Jack Lenihan drove him. It had seven punctures on the way to Ennis."

Mammy doesn't like war all the time. We listen to Vatican Radio which appeals for peace incessantly. Mammy says, "Let's kneel and pray for peace, The Pope has asked us." We go down on the drawing room's carpet and say the rosary for Pius XII's intentions, the first and last time us two Catholics did that. Do bad Catholics' prayers count?

The German boys were light, blonde and leaflike, gliding on canals on rippling water in magazines. The English boys were around you, coming out of the cider door, riding bashfully to hounds, coming into the yard ... dismounting wheatsheaf knights, going over on the boat for king and country; the German boys were leaving universities, duelling clubs, putting the image of the Virgin Mary inside their tunics, going to the depot, the camp, to the East. The English boys deprived of the mountain, the meadow, the walk across the downs, the theatre stall, transferred to the tank and the desert.

I heard it just happened on the bridge, at Woodenbridge, in the centre of the bridge, at midday, in the sight of the uncle's hotel: rosy-cheeked but otherwise pale Church of Ireland women—they came right up to him, a young man with all those non-throwaway medals clicking in the shadows behind him. There in their shiny gloves the white feathers. Ned Bailey. Up in the big house his father stirs uneasily, who had a part of Lower Egypt in his paws, in the hotel in the hill his uncle the major weeps unsteadily. Their heir, this man, will live inside their walls and trees, will be the god of the club underneath, one of the oldest in the country, small white balls drift in the wind. Jeeps will adore his hanging rutted road that winds up the dense woods.

Mammy has a big story after her night in Dublin; she was in the buttery of the Hibernian Hotel. Two armies without medals or arms came in by different doors. They take up positions on the polished counter with the gold and pink handles. When they have enough—not that, when it is near closing time—they imagine it is Christmas time, peace on earth, maybe Benedict XV's Christmas, Mammy's favourite

Pope, suspension of gun, smoke, and powder, singing danc-
ing and drinking along the line, marriage between the two
trenches, the Birth of Our Lord 1914. They move together
in the buttery, glasses clinking, pale ale not so pale, brandy
and rum dark and no stranger, none of it is rationed
tonight. Tom and Jerry, but officers only, with passes from
the camp in the neutral country, shaking hands which is an
act of high treason, kissing cousins who should be court-
martialled, Anglo-Saxon brothers. Wars end here, the jokes
are the same, same change for the drinks, arms on each
other's shoulders, medals not remembered, ten o'clock, time
of closure, one can not hold back, officers and gentlemen,
guests at a wedding that hadn't been held recently, tankards
of tribal reunion. Mates instead of fighters, the Kaiser and
the King are real cousins; let us embrace under the holy
leaves and wreaths of Christmas.

Benedict XV on his knees, his slight body, spent, racked
in prayer, in one chapel after another, begging the followers
of Christ not to kill each on the nativity. "We implore you
to listen to Us in your hearts. We think of the lambs that
are slaughtered hourly." Kaiser, King, their kingdoms, long
ago left the bells of the seven hills, those hills still dreaming
of Latin. Hymns begin. Officers take their revolvers out:
the singers are deserters. Padre, get out of our way, we'll
shoot the drunkards.

Mammy says wars would end if everyone started to drink
together. "Mammy, are you sure in Ireland?" "Yes, they
do that at the fairs and beat each other up. Still, if they
didn't drink too much, there would be peace. The Pope
has sent a message to us that we must say the Rosary every
day to the Queen of Peace." We fall to our knees in the
evening light. If Benedict couldn't do it, Pius won't be able.

Buick, my '39 Buick. White-tyred, such enormous sleekness,
bulk is grace as it sails through the chickens and donkeys

on the road, not patient with the cows who don't run into the hedges; we are super Americans in a super chariot. We stream to the races, to the beàch, to Poolaphuca before God the Government put it under water. We see the visiting Japanese destroyers in Dun Laoghaire harbour, or to the Sugarloaf on the last day cars are on the roads. The New World machine up on blocks behind the fading green doors of the garage. We would move back the doors and look at it, tired of the traps and bicycles in the yard and Daddy's simple Austin.

Hitler burnt on the ground and the Buick skips and jumps out of the shed. White tyres outside the District where we had been confined. Its first trip is on a call to Annagh, Daddy knows the way now, when he came first Ned Fogarty had to sit in the front seat and direct him. Ned didn't believe it would get down the roads and lanes.

Mammy and Daddy had gone to the Mayo Clinic for an internship, they had stayed over for the World's Fair, they bought it in a sale of models, one giant Easter lamb of a car. She wanted to go back to Ireland, he didn't, she thought the car would make him remember the trip. God saw it through the Customs at Plymouth, God knows how God did it. She had a U.S. passport, a temporary importation. It stayed in Kensington for a while; Daddy worked in a hospital, it went on a holiday to Devon, it saw Holyhead in the week of Molotov and Ribbentrop, it was in neutral green heaven. It displaced the Peugeots Daddy had always bought, one is stored in Kilkee.

Daddy can't keep up with Buick, it has to go. Is he tired of people's curiosity? They sell to a man from Carlow whose check bounces. The solicitor from Gorey gets the money by going to the man's mother and threatening her. In gratitude, they give Mr. McEvoy a silver lamp at Christmas.

Noreen's Tale

It's a long way to come from Dingle, but if you come from there via Cathal Brugha street, you know things they don't know on the street of Ballyferriter. Things to cook and things to think about cooking. Oh, the feast is here. Banquet time! Dr. and Mrs. Liddy are quiet, they have breakfast in bed, orange juice, coffee and toast, maybe a poached egg. It's different on Sundays, they come downstairs for a fry before Mass. They light a cigarette in bed, sometimes she talks to him. The doctor comes down about ten to the private patients waiting in the hall. The mistress is quiet, she never speaks much in the house, sometimes she mentions menus (she reads cook books but never practices), sometimes not even that.

A lot of times she goes into the study and plays on the piano. Chopin they call it; Nocturnes. She goes into the drawing room and reads. I see her with French books occasionally. She sits in the armchair, on the grate's left. They wear lovely clothes, I like the doctor's blue pinstriped suit, with white shirt, tie, and white handkerchief in breast pocket. Mrs. Liddy goes up to Dublin to buy new dresses in Madame Doran's. They eat well in the house, let's not talk about the drink. The desserts they make me do, I'm good at that, I think it was Cathal Brugha's mission to put women into the Constitution as refined sweets-makers. They like "Noreen's cake", that's a jam omelette that stands up in its own dish, it oozes jam, I don't know if Mrs. Liddy likes a cuisine based on jam but the doctor and the children scoop it up. They go mad over Bakewell pudding, Queen of Puddings made with raspberry jam and meringues folded in on top of the jam. The Pyrex dish is a great invention; the pastry is in the trellis fashion (serve with doilies).

I have heard Mrs. Liddy say that people think too highly of Charlotte Rousse.

The only time I saw my mistress go mad was when Sara broke the Waterford glass bowl that was in the centre of the mahogany dining room table. Lovely purple blue crystal, reflecting the light of two hundred years. Mrs. Liddy came back from Hoynes's Hotel and saw it in flitters in the sink. She fell into a terrible quiet rage; I think she almost died. She also liked her lustres, vases with hanging glass pendants. They were on the drawing room mantlepiece; the children were playing and started throwing cushions. One lustre fell to the floor, the carpet didn't save it. I rushed in, it was in little pieces, the children started crying. Mrs. Liddy was heart-broken again.

She loved giving dinner parties, she hated going to any. She usually started with lobster cocktail, or later on, Lobster Newburgh. She would send for oysters—I remember the name of the place well, The Weir, Kilcolgan—they would arrive in the station and the doctor collected them. A fisherman from Arklow in the kitchen opened them. There would be a joint of beef or maybe a pheasant, with bread stuffing. Then I would bring in my famous desserts.

There was an old oil painting of a naval vessel with sails on the wall. During the meal she would point to the stars and stripes flying from the rigging, she was proud of that. Less stars than now.

Clare Reeves Liddy, as she signed her cheques, in her fur coat from New York with a muffler, coming down the stairs, not saying goodbye, off to the Captain's dinner in Arklow. And hearing her returning so late, after enjoying herself, I often wonder how she got back, how she got the car in between the entrance pillars of the drive.

Molly's Tale

I know the big houses and the glens of Ireland. Our cottage at Auchavanagh was snug, it was hidden in the shadows of Lughnaquilla, it was snowy at times. The valley was a quiet place, there were a few families and many sheep and dogs. There was hardly any gentry. John Redmond's house that had been a barracks in '98 and then Parnell's hunting lodge; a shiny road up there, or a dull one, depending on your mood.

I began in the scullery of Johnny MacArdle, down the road a bit. The place was all ivy and kept lawns, and peacocks. At first in the houses I was in there were many cooks and helpers, then it came down to two and now one. People never stopped eating, I never stopped cooking: salads, cocktails, fowl, meat, sauces, game, vegetables ... mousses, rousses, trifles, puddings, chocolate, ice cream, stewed apples. A young mistress or master could be our friend, we would go in the orchard with them, or down the road to pick berries, or shop or picnic in the carriage or car. We protected them from their parents, we did not say what we thought of any of it. The young Vernons in Clontarf Castle played terrible tricks and I won't tell what they did sometimes. Some of us had to think on baby trouble.

I came to Coolgreany on a bicycle by the back roads, an old bike on a road like a cattle track, over the Wicklow Gap. I pedal home now and then on Sundays; God knows how much heather I pass by. They said I had rosy cheeks, I laugh through them. Old Mrs. Ellis was a terror to the girls, a tartar like the Queen, the ould one would keep the food locked up in the cupboards; she'd come down in the morning and write the menu for the day on a slate hanging near one of the basement windows. She'd measure the food and little would be laid out for us at lunch or dinner; only scraps. She was plentiful with apples, ould windfalls; Adam and Eve didn't eat all day in the garden except it was cider they were at.

Mrs. Ellis would poke into the bedroom, look under the door to see if there was any dust, same under the beds, us Catholics were dirty. The worst thing, getting up at four-thirty in the winter to heat the water for Mr. Ellis's bath. We'd pour it in the bath and he'd go past us to get in without grunting a "thank you." Percy Cudlipp was the chauffeur. As they were getting into the car he would take off his cap and put the rugs over them. At the Eucharistic Congress in 1932 the village put a banner across the street, they never went that way into Arklow anymore, they'd always go by the Inch road.

Then I came to the Liddys, and bustle. All day in the kitchen, feed the family, throw something to the dogs, look after Tom, maybe Peter, in the yard; the patients ringing the bell and passing down the hall; every time you had to do something on the cooker the bell went; my sister-in-law, the Dispensary woman, looking over my shoulder to see what's coming in, what's boiling. Mrs. Liddy different at certain times, wanting her lunch at one, supper at six-thirty, you'd prepare the best dinner for her but she'd come in two hours late and it would be burnt in the oven, she'd been out maybe with Paddy Barrett or that Una Brennan in the Golf Club or at Courtown. She'd say, as she passed the fridge on the way to the sitting room, "I want a scotch."

I always loved the children, I loved Jimmy. We had a terrible fight in the kitchen, one worse than usual when I walked out up the street to my house and I said I would never come back. Your father and mother were out in Woodenbridge. You came up the street after me, crying your eyes out, holding on to my white coat, saying you were sorry. How fond of me you were, saying you loved me as much as your Mammy. That time in Kilkee, when your mother wanted to stay till September, I wanted to bring my husband down. Good boy that you were, you went into the drawing room where you used to play golf, pretending the holes in the carpet were holes, to ask your mother. I was outside on the sea wall my hair going in all directions and you told me she said no.

Nanny's Tale

Dr. Liddy was an old segosha. He didn't collect bills he was owed, when a farmer asked him how much he owed, he'd say, "Whatever you think." He was with Mr. Weadick on Thursdays, they would drive up to the Dispensary at Wicklow Gap. Mr. Weadick was the Social Insurance man from Arklow; he got married late. Mr. Weadick sat in the car with a pile of anonymous letters on his lap. I used to make tea while he would be waiting to go down to the doctor's office. Once he brought in a piece of chicken breast; you knew he got it from one of the hotels in Arklow. He had it with his tea. I thought I would be offered part of it. I was never so much as offered a taste, and he kept up coming to me after that. He used to keep his counsel, but he argued with Dr. Liddy who used to sign any form and give a man the benefit of the doubt.

> To Dr. Liddy
> and Mr. Weadick if
> Johnny Manning is
> getting the money or
> tickets from you he is
> working every day since
> this time last year
> does all the fairs driving to
> and from and done all
> the threshings last year
> and this year it's not fair to
> others. Paying insurance and
> was cut off in a few weeks
> he gets 10 shillings and one pound
> a day it's not fair other men
> didn't get off working
> and doing the cod

with you and Mr.
Weadick he has
lots of made up lies
to tell you's,
A Friend

Johanna's Tale

Dr. Liddy didn't like Mrs. Conway, but he put up with Johnny Murphy. She was for ever sending for the doctor and Johnny was forever getting married and asking advice about women. When her husband was only a week dead, Johnny came to Maggie's door at night and whispered through it, "I'm sorry for your trouble, would you think of getting married again?" Once Dr. Liddy was trying to get off Johnny Murphy's first wife when she was going to be due. She wasn't being helpful so he said, "can't you ask your husband?" She replied, "He wouldn't know something like that, he wouldn't be good at it." Dr. Liddy replied, "On your way back through Ballyfad stop in the Post Office and ask Mrs. Conway, she'll know."

Johnny Murphy was married three times—his first two wives were hitched before and were buried with their first husbands. He wanted to be buried with at least one wife. The doctor didn't mind him, but Mrs. Conway was different. He only answered Inch 6 up to two o clock. Mrs. Conway wore bulbous hats like they did in the forties. In summer she would drive to Courtown on a Sunday and look at the crowds, she never looked in the direction of the sea. She got one of her children to get her an ice cream. She never got out of the car.

Bill's Tale

We used to play skittles on the road in Gurteen. They were all set up, and then we'd hear the sound of the car being started in the yard at Coolgreany. We would have them out of the way before the doctor's car got near them at all.

Aine's Tale

It's funny what sticks in a child's mind. I remember the doctor, a big man, he never done one thing everyone did at Mass. He never genuflected.

Seamus's Tale

Mary Neil was taken ill, and Mick Shortall went down to the doctor's house at about one a.m. and banged on the door. There was a lot of banging and the doctor's head finally came out of the window, "Devil, what the blazes is going on?" Mick Shortall said, "Mary Neil is very ill," "What's wrong with her?" "She's dead, doctor." "What the bloody hell can I do about it?" The window closed and fastened.

Sean's Tale

The night the Germans bombed Arklow, Mrs. Shortall came out of her house and blessed the people with holy water. Nanny Byrne was asking me to go into Arklow, "How is Doll," she was dazed. Doll was working for Dr. Hamilton at the time. Dr. Liddy came out and said it was over, they could see what happened in the morning, but not to go near the bombs, "If you have drink in the house open it." Trouble was, none of us had. We wouldn't listen, we ran in the woods, Ellis's and Brooks's. If there had been caves gone into them, if there had been druids we'd have knelt to them.

Billy Wicklow's Tale

When my father died I decided to open Shelton as a hotel. I had some bad memories of it though I loved the walks along the Avoca river, the rose garden laid out by my mother who died so long ago We did well having the Taoiseach Mr. Costelloe, and Desmond FitzGerald in his last dying months, I'm afraid. Guy Burgess paid us a visit and got drunk on the lawn; this was the first time I met Dr. Liddy who had difficulty telling Burgess's mother his condition. The Liddys came a lot to dinner, ten and sixpence table d'hôte, the children made fun of our savoury Angels on Horseback.

They laughed when my old nurse called out, "Billy, have you done your hair?" Mrs. Liddy alerted them, she was a good-looking American. I decided to have a club room for locals, and Barbara and Ted Elton arranged it in the library. The merchants, lawyers, doctors flocked to it, Des French, the Brennans, specially Arthur, a cavalry chap if ever there was one, the McDowells, the Fogartys, and young Kavanagh of the cinemas who was attentive to Clare Liddy. They drank Pimm's Cup, though it wasn't strong enough for them: Evelyn Waugh and Betjeman, who were at Shelton before the war, would have found it amusing.

I gave a talk on Tom Moore at The Royal Hotel. A drunken woman started heckling me the moment we arrived at the subject of Tom Moore and Bermuda. The Liddys and I drank some whiskey in a private room; the doctor introduced his son who wanted to go into publishing. I warned it was a difficult business to get into. I thought to myself I have given away a fortune to Clonmore & Reynolds, to help the Roman Church on earth.

When down I attended last Mass in Arklow, and then a jorum of gratitude in the other hotel, Hoyne's.

Jim's Tale

I live halfway between Arklow and the village and I've seen The Liddys drive by for years in their different cars. I've suffered from good health most of my life and only been to the doctor's twice.

I was talking to Bobby the other night. He was in the kitchen one night in Shelton, with Barbara Elton. Champagne, he said, they were drinking. Billy—I call him the young fella—came in and Bobby stood up to him and said, "I'm a Kavanagh, when are you going to give us back our lands?" Next night they met in the clubroom and he first thing the young fella said was, "Mr. Kavanagh, what are you drinking?"

The young fella was a writer and I'll tell you something about him: he'd fill half a glass with olive oil and then by god he could drink three quarters of a bottle of whiskey.

I love old Kilbride, there's one of them in there. New Kilbride, that's not the same, but do you know what? I travel the length and breadth of a few counties and anywhere I pass a cemetery I lift my hat and say a few prayers. I do it often outside New Kilbride, you see the young fella is in there.

It nearly killed them, back before the war, when he turned. The old fellow wouldn't permit him in Shelton at weekends in case he'd be seen going to Mass. He was a Church of England clergyman in England, he held a service in New Kilbride, did you know that?

I remember the old fellow well, the seventh earl. He used to go round in a trap with a gray mare. They had the best land in Ireland—Sheepwalk.

Victor's Tale

Shelton was a lovely old place. The gardens were kept perfect, exactly the same way the first Countess had left them. There was King James's Walk, he stayed here after the Battle of the Boyne. And the remains of an old bridge in the river!

I met Mrs. Liddy over there sometimes in the day and once she asked to show her where exactly the main part of the Battle of Arklow had taken place.

Most of the carnage happened just off the new Main Road as you leave town, where Quinnsworth is now. It was a British officer that saved the croppies. After the battle Lord Wicklow's militia was going to finish them off.

Tom's Tale

I was in love with Clare Reeves Liddy. I was a braggart, how many I had in bed. I used to go out to Coolgreany to drink in the top bar, where my father used to serve before we hit the jackpot. I often went down to the house, sometimes with Des French. He was in love with her someway too, the way a queer man can be with a beautiful woman! I was jealous of James Liddy as I was never jealous of another man.

We Brennans, we were the Don Juans. Don Nuzum called his horse Don Juan one time. I rode it at point-to-points.

I had T.B. and went to Switzerland, and boasted about the nurses. I used to have dreams about Clare out there, high in the mountains.

The Last Tale

You are very much on my mind.

You enjoyed life but you didn't allow for enjoyment. Anything serious I ever did is because love is and cannot be taught. Handed on as we looked at each other and drank, or didn't fill the glass, just gazed over newspapers or our reading. Love is not imprisonment or being caged; it is capture. Not that even, perhaps rapture and some decent temporary exit. Engender a soul and don't sell it right now.

Things I would like to send you now. Uncle James was on the committee of Irish-Americans who gave money to honour Yeats's old age, he funded Joseph Campbell's chair at Fordham, he read Finnegans Wake in 1939. I would like to send you the 1939 cover of Time with Joyce's picture on it subtitled, "He wrote Hawthorne's dream book." Do you remember reading that? The only time I ever talked to James's son, "young Dan," who is famed for owning the Los Angeles Rams, he asked me did I think Joyce was on dope when he wrote the wake book? Isn't a drop in the glass enough for a look back?

In the issue is Dev's picture, and the report on Ireland states that cinema audiences in Dublin used to clap when Adolf Hitler's image came on screen. Did you witness that?

Enquiries for you!

There is no other womb after the first one, there is no other Catholic Church after it begins. There is love after the first love, but unless you are lucky it may just be friendship. No Mass, after the first high one.

The Wexford Opera Festival

Daddy has another hobby these days besides golf. Mammy is mad about it, she minds Daddy being down in Wexford though she doesn't want to go herself. It started with local gramophone recitals, and its origin lies with Compton MacKenzie—Daddy and his Wexford friends call him Monty—nice whiskered old smoothie of the Queen Mother's dared them into it, "If you are so interested in Opera why don't you have a festival." Tom Walsh, he used to like Mammy, becomes the action man. Festival of three doctors, late night Italian starlets singing upstairs in White's, the Staffords sitting around like decorated tugboats, Fintan O'Connor dearly loving a lord who's in tow (he prefers Longford to Wicklow, cream buns easier to deal with than whiskey). Des French has money, I think he still likes Mammy, he's been going to Italy for years star-listening. Tom goes there to pick performers: Milan must be a big Wexford.

It's a big fancy dress ball down here, on and off stage. It allows the Anglo-Irish time to forget about horses. The opera is La Sonnambula, 18th/19th centuries cusp fluff, Marilyn Cotlow is sleep-walking and singing, Monti the tenor is awake and marvellous. Having dinner in the Talbot, Mammy is a little smashed in protest, she said she wouldn't come, then she did—smells the fish, it's bad; the wine is corked, sent back. I smell perfume from dressed-up men at the next table, they're made-up like MacLiammoir at Jammet's. Daddy says there's the Queen's cousin Lord Harwood whose wife is a pianist, the other Desmond Shaw-Taylor something to Lady Gregory. Daddy and I walk to the opera, Mammy to the hotel.

Wexford is near, by the sea, and produces beautiful appearances. I feel sleepy in the Theatre Royal, do I snore or do I dream I snore? A tall, thin man on the other side of Daddy is sound asleep, Daddy sighs and we try to manoeuvre over his long legs at the interval. Daddy tells me that's Lennox Robinson, Yeats's partner at the Abbey Theatre—Yeats now that's my interest, and Mammy's too.

On the other hand, the real Ireland.

It was June 29, the feast of SS. Peter and Paul. In O'Rafferty's next door, the proprietor Vincey had won the jackpot on the last four races at the Curragh. He made £6,000. The door to the lounge was locked and Vincey, piano accordion strapped to his chest, stood in front of it and sang snatches of songs, a bar or two, or maybe a verse, interrupting himself to dash madly around to say something, to me between "It's a long way to Tipperary" and "The Croppy Boy", "you have the brains, Jimmy, you'd know about it," or "I'll be in to see the mammy on Tuesday, the car broke down," and off again to song and people milling about dancing and swinging in groups or couples, with Benny, the ex seminarian, the brother, a cap over his eyes repeating, "I was only the messenger" (he brought the bet to the bookie on the course), and a young man in a cap and tie throwing the cap to the ceiling when the song told him to do that—over and over in a famous radio voice gave us the closing laps of the race.

2
Dublin

The Pub

The first pub, away from the pub that is home, and the pubs around home. The pub away from the dens of U.C.D. students. The third home, if you have a job. The Estates General. The Third Estate, journalists and part-timers. Tick haven of poets. Curragh Camp of Republicans. Perhaps The House of Lords, that is what Patrick Kavanagh calls it: "There's Lord Brady in mid-oration," meaning one of his friends from the Blackrock Tailoring around the corner who had cut the telephone wires to the Magazine Fort in the Park on the night the boys raided, and around too on the night they heaved up equestrian George II in the Green. Neither the old I.R.A. is here nor the new, on stools the mid-I.R.A. who partook in the mid-life crisis of the State. The Irish of O Cadhain, the bawdiness of Behan circulate here, nostalgias from the Glasshouse cells. The first start can be the market pubs, or the dock pubs; let us rise and praise the Lord at dawn, let us see if he will help us post-date a cheque. High ceiling, stained glass window, colour photograph of Fishermen's Wharf, worn red seating, semi-circular snug at left to side of counter, tiny lounge to the back differentiated by a pillar, men down steps, women up stairs, side door to a lane where nefarious deeds may happen. After "Time Gentlemen, please" banging Paddy O' Brien, Jimmy McDaid, Noel, in old white coats, escort you to the pavement: heaven and then you become cold Purgatory ghost, except there is an after life in a brown paper bottle in the direction of someone's house.

The Day the Martello Tower Opened

A skinny and shiny day, the 1960's are starting.

The Triestine bells of Sant' Antonio Taumaturgo ring in our ears. St. Martin is testing the Christ in him by giving one half of his cloak to a beggar man. St. Joan of Arc is fitting on a pair of trousers and testing her blade, the venerable Columba Marmion is testing a light Belgian beer.

Trieste remains coffee houses, newspapers, a sloping park strewn with busts of authors and tables where Umberto Saba, the place's poem teller, waits for the waiter and thinks of the other one that sits there, Dublin's exile shadow. Port cities of empire's dream.

Then the bell ceases. The sun rises on Dublin Bay to con-firm this day when the world expands in a series of flushes and blobs, winks and jests. The drink of the morning, the roads to it are sharp, white. The dark shades of the body's night prepared for it.

Down by the water, before you get to the Napoleon-seeing brick of the tower, there's a patch of thick grass in front of a house. You hear the cicada chirping in your ears. What does the thirsty cicada breeze on about? It replies from its porch to the sun. You think you heard Stephen Dedalus's voice once that afternoon, "The world is more straight and Protestant than you imagine."

The sun rises on Dublin Bay as well as on Galway Bay, and does that bow to the cicadas?

Bells on our fingers, bells or boils elsewhere, as before the strident epiphany on the grass we drive through Monkstown and Blackrock; Dermot Bouchier-Hayes driving Mary Lavin in a red Triumph sports car in front. We park and talk, imagine how local and exotic Dedalus was in the morning's pub, and enter.

The great Parisian ladies, Sylvia Beach and Maria Jolas, rest in deck chairs at the foot of the iron stairs. Alcohol is being poured by the glad Irish hand; we have come rather late, we worry about supply. I get a glass of whiskey in my hand but Bertie Rodgers loosens it from my grasp while talking slowly and elegantly. Dominic Behan runs by us, incredibly drunk, Brendan is reported missing. The host Michael Scott slips out of his house, a palace of modernity white and gleaming, to take guests down to the forty foot. I see Frank O'Connor and Louis MacNeice coming back up the rocks without agility, for some reason a ragged looking pair. Mary Lavin knows everyone, conversation over the place.

I hie down to that necessary relief, the nearest pub. In Fitzgerald's a selection of the motley has taken their seats and glasses. MacNeice rumbles in a corner and walks off towards the jakes. He is followed by a collection of Jesuit-English-teacher-erudite schoolboys from Gonzaga, I plunge after them. MacNeice thunders as he pisses, "Poetry is on the floor." The boys try to engage him, I engage them, one of them is called Paul Durcan aged seventeen. The second coming was almost at hand, as it often is.

I was the second curator of the tower, Michael Hartnett was the third, I got him the job. Michael used to invite his girl friend to a sleeping bag on the floor of the museum, in the morning they would wash in the pools among the rocks, Dedalus and nymph. The body white like the start of a pint. I was an inefficient curator, once I forgot to lock up, once I kept Vera and Igor Stravinsky waiting at the gate, coming out late by bus from Kavanagh in McDaid's. The sun kept coming up, and Dedalus was, and is, the party of us all. That party has never ended in my lifetime. Remission of sins without end. Whatever pours. The dark night of the soul must be the daylight of the body.

John Jordan

Sean O'Sullivan the painter, big rosy cheeks, raspy voice, whispered to any gentleman who sat on a stool near him, "Shall I compare thee to a Summer's day, Thou art more lovely and more temperate." A gentleman in his hearing gave his poems to Patrick Kavanagh for commentary, they had turned into The Sonnets. Shakespeare was everywhere, riding his bicycle down streets broad and narrow. Who else would have let Cupid and quiver blow in over us? The young barman, Noel, was pricked. John Jordan presided over McDaid's Court of Love with the remorse of a classical literary critic.

It does not seem polite to discuss love, but what else to whisper about in a pub, since it makes poetry its slave. John extolled a counter phrase, "The holiness of the heart's affections." "What about its disaffections?" we objected.

John had fallen in love with the same person to make me jealous. We held stormy picnics in the small lounge. "Don't you dare to do that to me," dialogue as we sped in my car to Austin Clarke's in Templeogue. "I am interested," John said, "in peace and quiet." "I am interested in love and quiet," I said. John replied, "I am not like you, I do not want to do it, because you see it is a sin." I rejoined, "There are a lot of corpses around in the Freudian sense— is it a sin to touch a corpse, to bring it to life?" "For the life of me, I can't see why you are never serious."

We stopped before the door of an unornate man, we had in our charge a bottle of Bristol Cream.

We waited while the bottle was taken. It stood a while on a table dreaming. Nora Clarke took it, brought it back with sandwiches. The good sour poet liked good sweet sherry. Austin talked quietly, not stand-offish, a sigh over Dublin sorrows. But it was never a place to discuss love, at least not that of the same sex melt. He had resigned from the Academy of Irish Letters, "They gave the Gregory Medal to that foppish fellow MacLiammoir." On the other malefactor, Kavanagh, who had stood for The Reich at wartime gatherings, Austin remarked he had seen him, momentarily, on television in a dark tunnel pub on Dame Street.

From his room, laden with review copies, he hovered us to the door, "The greatest comfort is to have a car like that, not to have to take the bus." John and I settled down to talk about reviewing on the way into town. I said it was lucky John had made his contribution before the word "brilliant" got picked. John countered that he remembered the time when nobody put the question, "What are you writing now?"

Bon viveur! Blessed is he who exports through his actions wine and roses, for he shall receive T.B. John became ensconced at the James Connolly Memorial Hospital in Blanchardstown. His room had a balcony where occasionally a replica of his past might be seen sunning himself. John was welcoming in pyjamas and pallor. I drove Kavanagh to see him; I drove the venerable collectivist Peadar O'Donnell there. John knew everything. he liked everyone, whether it was O'Donnell hearing the valleys sing or Kavanagh turning his back on the singing valleys.

I got to know the car park well.

John as usual confided about God. "Human sexuality is God's most complex gift. Once you have it, what do you do with it? How do you fit it into your prayer life?"

John's charity was extensive; he sent a pound a week to the young poet Michael Hartnett.

I carried the suitcase and books as John left the James Connolly. He was reading *Essays and Introductions*. "His prose is that of a wonderful old fruit," he said. "Yeats turned the twilight into wine-fake clothes. Sparkling camp from the Autumn of the body to the Summer of a Blueshirt. Couture."

In the car, John continued, "There are two kinds of dead. Pagan sensual dead satisfied as in the dreams of Yeats, and our dead the Church kind who hope to rise..." I drove him over the hump-backed canal bridge at Harrold's Cross, we passed by the Posts and Telegraphs kiosk at the corner of the road leading to Park Avenue, "Michael and Hilton both used to say I lived in a telephone booth."

I took the big step, I invited John for the weekend, to my parents' house. John said his father came from Wexford. He put on his hacking clothes, he was proud of them, he mentioned them on each stop on the way down. In the pub next to my house he kept on getting in the way of the dart players. He did not notice. His main statement became, "I demand to be taken to Mass." In the night he ranged through the house, gliding into snoring bedrooms suddenly awake. He stood on the landing, he beckoned down the stairs, "I demand a glass of milk." He lay in the grey room in the morning, "John, it's time for last Mass." The gaunt deacon on the edge of the bed smiled, "Child, bring me a large brandy."

We drove by the back road, the Slatequarry road, to the Woodenbridge Hotel. He insisted he was a Roman Catholic. "You see, Child, I enjoy doing it, it gives me too much pleasure, it is unlawful. Anyway, God does not like it." My riposte, "I am frightened of sex, though I love the idea of it."

He said he had been to the Woodenbridge Hotel before, at the butt of the fertile literary valley, at its head Tom Moore's Tree and nearby Major Bayley's wooded hill where Frank O'Connor's wife gathered spinach for dinner. John had gone there with Paddy Swift, the painter. They had read Ulysses. In that text of champagne, liberation. In that barn it was bliss to be alive and naked.

How We Stood Our Rounds:
Bohemian Dublin in the Sixties

We have Proust's words for it, backed up by Beckett, that
voluntary memory does not hold a candle or a glass to the
involuntary kind as a means of evocation. But for me
involuntary memory is not a rare experience, as far as the
sheeny life of Dublin is concerned. We indomitable
Irishry are consumed with spontaneous reminiscences,
and this can turn into a tasteless gift at the heart of our
culture. Yet there seems something occult, as well as
native, in unquenchable, unforsakeable, but unbidden
re-enactment of the past–texts pour quelque chose. "When
I grew up" is always coming to an end; it never ends. I
have wanted to ask W.B. Yeats, is not the answer to your
refrain "What then" "Then again" or even "Finn again." I
would like to interrogate this shade, how many times have
Egypt, Greece, and Rome died, and come back again?

For a reading of the burial of the fifties and sixties Dublin,
I refer to the comment of the art critic of the Irish Times
on the death of the painter Patrick Collins, on March, 2,
1994. Brian Fallon says of Collins, "He also mixed easily
with poets and writers generally, and was central in the
now vanished Dublin bohemia which included Patrick
Kavanagh and many more." "Now vanished" the perfect
undertaker's phrase. One has to note in Fallon's obituary
how Kavanagh preempts other literary figures. As he often
comically and proudly narrated, he was the god of that scene.

I met him in the middle fifties as he was transferring from café
to bar. I recollect him here oddly with two other personages
of that scene who were my friends, Liam Miller and
Anthony Kerrigan. I say "oddly" because there was never
eye to eye agreement between Kavanagh and the others.

Paddy was the rural-born presentation, inheritor of Yeats's reduced but updated hazel wand; Miller with his press championed the other claimant, Austin Clarke, and fashioned the succession; and Kerrigan was a Christopher Columbus who arrived on our shore to find the literary set he had partly imagined.

Tony Kerrigan was a laureate translator. He put Miguel de Unamuno into English, a seven volume collected works. He did five books of Jorge Luis Borges, fiction and poetry. He gave the English-speaking world Reinaldo Arenas's *El Central* and his most successful venture was his version of Camilo Jose Cela's *The Family of Pascal Duarte* a Goyaesque portrait of minimal domesticity. Kavanagh received his first large grant shortly before his death, and three years before his Kerrigan received from the National Endowment for the Arts a senior fellowship in literature and $40,000. He was, of course, a poet in both his languages, Castilian and English; without that he would not have been a laureate translator. Not the least part of him was his manner of pre-war bohemian—apocalyptically ready, brazenly ready to go, ready to interfere in the affairs of the great; disturbed but craftily and lucidly so. I noticed the resemblance between John Berryman and Kerrigan when they joined forces, in Dublin's chaotic afternoons and early nights, and charged. They gave no quarter, at least not to themselves. They were aficionados of Ireland—under the stars of Joyce and Yeats. They felt they were among their own people, a presumption vigorously disputed by Kavanagh and his nativist court in McDaid's. This did not compromise the fun Kerrigan, Berryman, and Miller had near the banks of the Grand Canal. Dublin is a one-poet town, it was Kavanagh's moment, they didn't care, they had another one.

Driven by the whimsy of being born from an Irish-sounding father in an American-sounding place, the Canal Zone,

Tony arrived with his wife Elaine at the yellow brick tower of Stephen Dedalus and walked up the winding Buck Mulligan staircase. Zero Mostel had just been there casting Leopold Bloom's voice up the chimney. Tony, myopically eloquent under youthfully fringed white hair, prayed at the stations of the waistcoat, the cane, and the death mask. I was late that day opening the tower, delayed by the hardy business of poem-buying from Kavanagh in McDaid's, for my new magazine *Arena*. We had concluded with "luck money" and a handshake.

I was the summer curator of Joyce's Martello Tower. It had just been opened in the full shine of the sixties; the nation was full of delicious backward glances. Kavanagh spoke as the laureate of the present, "Write about that pint on the table in front of you." He stayed at McDaid's during business hours; the Kerrigans were staying at the Four Courts Hotel, we agreed to meet that night. We did, and bumped into a magical umbrella holder for two generations in Irish literature: Miller of the Dolmen Press, a genial rusher about town. Conspiracies of another Renaissance! The world was a new lounge bar then, and we crossed over from the Dolmen office on Baggot Street to Phil Ryan's upstairs. We were in thick with the bartender, Peter— Tipperary so loud and clear—by luck he was serving the Ulster poet Bertie Rodgers who, between barnaps, had a monologue about Estyn Evans, the anthropologist. The Kerrigans blinked, smiled at Bertie's plus fours, took a drink, joined the circle. At late closing time we danced through the trees in the middle of the road to the whiskey bottle and the array of Eric Gill's books and bookplates in Miller's glass case. For Tony Kerrigan it was a fable comparable to the one he was talking about—the eight hours of Picasso talking and drawing while Cela looked on like a cat. I heard Oscar Wilde's whisper to me, "Life is the nights after the opening night."

All the nights after that. I was playing a dangerous game cohorting with folks Kavanagh didn't like, I could have lost my right-hand seat in McDaid's. It was part of my prancing time; American academics did the Baggot promenade: Max Rosenthal in bow tie, quiet John Unterecker in the café above the Brown Jacket bookshop, quieter David Krause haunting Miller. On the same stretch Kavanagh would hail me advancing from Parsons bookshop towards Harry Street, "What news, foreign or domestic?" Frank O'Connor, wife and pram, would trundle down the street; Kavanagh would wait patiently in a doorway until they had passed.

Ireland is one pub, and friendship is one lounge. No one is ever there without a drink in hand. A melody of lights and brights. Buzz in a labyrinth (and thinking of old and new Spains, were Gerard Brennan, V.S. Pritchett, and Octavio Paz the same time ghost?). Tony and Elaine, their son Camilo Jose—Cela was his compadre—and their daughter Antonia had moved into the top floor of a house in Fitzwilliam Square, to which was added a week later a white Mercedes down below on the street. Were there enough coins on the mantlepiece to put petrol into it?

We all thought the Baggot Street summer would be endlessly renewed. There would be nods to libations and gods. John Berryman slid down the bannister of the morning stairs of the Majestic Hotel, as Liam Miller and I called. At the foot of the stairs he hopped into the bar—without a word. A bottle of gin was placed in front of him and it would be a few minutes before he'd talk. Our manifest poetries stood up, circled around us on the dance floor. Mine was of the bog flower ephebe, "boy" was interchangeable with "girl" in the singing lines. Tony Kerrigan's rousingly male:

> The clatter bones are puky bones
> compared to Mary Jordan's bones

which shimmer in her milky hands
like milkmaid's making-morning hands.
And still I live in hopes to see
the Holy Ground once more.

Kerrigan would get down on his knees and forget the
Bollingen Foundation, for which he worked, whenever he
saw Mary Jordan or her like. He would worship her hands
that made music, her fingers on silver spoons bearing
oranges or leafing figs: "Fine Girl You Are!"

I made a betrayal. I gave Paddy my sister Nora's address
and he would come knocking on her door. As his poems
show he liked medical women students, they would look
after his old age. I remember him whispering to one in a
McDaid's corner, "I'll take you to New York and we'll
buy the ring in Tiffany's." He took Nora several times to
afternoon tea in the Shelbourne and paid. He invited her
to go to America with him. When various personages—
Billy Wicklow, James Pope Hennessy, to speak of the
dead—passed by the tea table, Kavanagh would say, "A
woman has nothing to fear from that man."

Kerrigan was the cavalier in attendance on Liam Miller,
which allowed Tony tilt in the whiskey whirlwind with
that gracious playboy of The Eastern World. When wives
were far away, we screeched in cars or cabs on bad tires
through the backlanes of the Irish Sea. Once we had a girl
whose proudest boast was that her uncles had drunk five
farms in Tipperary. She lay on the taxi floor when we
passed a possible prying uxorious window. Miller and I
were content with porter on non-whiskey nights; Tony
wanted oysters and porter.

Kavanagh, exiled over a bounced cheque from McDaid's
(common practice—but the owner unexpectedly came
downstairs and confronted the head barman with it) sat in

The Bailey looking out the window. He watched a notable Dublin figure being escorted by Miller and Kerrigan and spat out, "Christ crucified between two thieves." He never threw a word to Kerrigan—it would have been, Yankee, go back to Palma—but there was a reconciliation with the Dolmen Press. I joined the publisher and the poet on Baggot Street bridge; the publisher had the camera which provided the photographs for Kavanagh's *Self Portrait*. As we went down to the canal bank, architectural students on the almost completed roof of the Bord Fáilte building cheered. Kavanagh gave his G.A.A. referee's smile.

On the St. Stephen's Green corner with Leeson St., over a grocery and opposite a student pub, Edward Dahlberg, Tony's exalted master, waited for us. A cave occupied by Plato and Aladdin shone. He had two handmaidens in there, his Irish woman Julia and New York woman Renee. As Elaine, Tony and I went up we heard the great boom, "I'm as lusty a Jew as Saul of Tarsus." Dahlberg was the first person I had met who wrote exactly as he pounded the universe; even Kavanagh only swung at it. Dahlberg was a 19th century dream and nightmare, wearing a nightshirt and stocking cap outfit he sat in his armchair. We were ministered to with glasses of wine; Julia and Renee withdrew. Edward thundered on Gareth Browne and other "señoritos" of the peerage; Tony and Elaine pondered this talk of friendship with a young man and its golden alleyways. I thought of the uselessness of reincarnating ourselves in the young. The two "mujeres" walked about the house.

In the room, the hallway, the kitchen, were several thousand books soon to be crated for Mallorca or Rivington Street on the Lower East Side. As I progressed at intervals to the bathroom, I found the women having their own colloquium on the edge of the bath. Renee was talking about Henry

James. "You girls, having your own drinking party," I said and thought—a better "milagro" than what was happening in the sitting room.

In the Kerrigan apartment, on the top of a Fitzwilliam Square house, there seemed a lot of space with very white walls; you would expect the Mediterranean sparkle outside the windows. Elaine brought in a tray with sizzling tapas. How I loved riñones a la Jerez. On the couch Tony and Dahlberg jerkily conversed, the two Bollingen Foundation buddies, the silversmith and the goldsmith. Julia's head was hanging down; all was not well, conspiracy surged. Tony had been talking too many pills and vinos and they were trying to persuade him to go to Dean Swift's House of Rest, St. Patrick's Hospital. They had tried the day before, but by the time the cavalcade of two cars had got to the entrance gate, Admissions was closed. The curtains were drawn in Swift's House.

Tony seemed unplugged from the scene. Elaine was focusing on how to keep Dahlberg out of it. I am providential as I escort Julia and her towering, overcoated, husband down the stairs. Dahlberg's white hair and grey mustache preside over brooding in the Pembroke Bar. Sipping and sighing over glasses of stout, we lament the world's end, the fall of Troy and Washington, D.C. This expatriate, the protegé of D.H. Lawrence, the friend of Hart Crane watching waiter-fights in the Dome, shifts to more recent and familiar ground: Charles Olson, the Neptune of the Massachusetts coast, whom Dahlberg wants to dispatch.

"Olson's mother was an Irish biddy. When I used to stay in her house she always gave him the better cuts of meat. Right in front of us she put less on my plate.... *Call Me Ishmael* is my book, I wrote it for him. Where is the mention of my name? There is a dedication to me—on page 51!"

Tony Kerrigan wrote me a postcard from St. Pat's—did they have them for sale in the front office?—proclaiming yellow is the colour of madness. I belonged to another religious persuasion and was saying my Office under McDaid's stained glass. McDaid's was numinous—a right number of priests, a certain set of vestments. There was Benediction in the early evening followed by private devotions. Beside Kavanagh, John Jordan was often the celebrant. "Blessed be God in His angels and in his saints." To whom exactly were we referring? We were not quite awash in Rilke's ghosts. The day's litanies were long, the congregation tired. From noon to roughly eight, Paddy was enthroned Coadjutor. In an occasional rest from his duties: he would slip out to a betting shop, or for a lamb chop in a nearby restaurant—but he was not pleased to be seen eating.

The language of the premises was Irish-rural.
"It's five pounds to talk to me today."
"Paddy, it's usually only a pound, even on a bad day."
"But it's a black day for me—hand over or fuck off."

I held up a one pound note. Paddy took it and savagely, if calmly, tore it to little pieces.

Some gent got down on his knees, and, in that small lounge behind the single pillar, scooped the green remnants up. It now hangs, framed and described, on a suburban wall.

The poet's bacchic discourse, contrasted with the "reasonableness" of the Kerrigan/Miller libations, occurred in other dissension centres. Paddy consumed Scotch and balanced it with baking soda in his hand for his stomach's sake. He kept on making strong points: he quoted the wisdoms of Pound; in Mooney's of Baggot Street he quoted Samuel Johnson on friendship, "A man should stretch his legs under the table," but I was running off to see Pat Clancy or friends. When he was staying in a nearby hospital, but on parole in Mooney's, I showed him a photograph of Thomas Kinsella in *Time* magazine. It was not the way to treat a sick man. To make up for it, I took a brown paper parcel of Guinness to his hospital ward. He was sitting at a table in front of the fire. He took out a bottle and drank it; he remarked his records were so interesting the doctors were sending them to Harvard.

Dissension centres were also frenzy areas. On Merrion Row we ran into Liam Miller and Katherine Graham, proprietor of *The Washington Post*. A fracas between Graham and Kavanagh broke out in the back room of O'Donoghues. Miller left, bowed by the loss of opportunities for Irish writers in the United States. In O'Neills, also in Merrion Row, Kavanagh whispered to me, "You're bent, but you're not as bent as Jordan." Kavanagh came to the Gorey Fleadh Ceoil in 1962; in French's Ice Cream Parlour Tom Kinsella was offering a drink to Leland Bardwell, Gareth Browne, everyone in the group, but Kavanagh growled, "I wouldn't take a drink from you." When Kinsella bought the round, Kavanagh interjected, "He wouldn't buy one for me." He demanded I take him out to my house in Coolgreany; my mother said no. He wrote up the situation in the Farmer's Journal—"turned away like a dog." After he disappeared for the night I found him, he wanted to go back to Dublin. I drove him as far as the Dargle Tavern in Bray; then he said he wanted to return to Gorey; I left him outside that pub door. To this day I can point out the roadside spots where we stopped for the operations of nature.

Then Kerrigan made his excursion to Gorey which had followed Wexford, the county seat, and created its own extraordinary festival. Paul Funge, an original because the Faust type is so unusual in Ireland, had assembled ideas and painters, writers, scene-shifters, choruses, and revellers. The pace thickened, the nights were bathed in longer light; and Diarmuid O Suilleabhain—novelist, poet, teacher in the Christian Brothers School—joined the traffic and critiqued the rest of the throng. Kerrigan saw O Suilleabhain as the soul and medicine man of the culture, and stepped up his formidable courtship powers. The attraction was O Suilleabhain, as a Gaelic poet and prose writer he had a number of publications and awards. Alastair Reid had impressed on Tony how an article on the fortunes of modern Gaelic would interest *The New Yorker*. Then Kerrigan discovered the Gaelic writer to be a tango dancer like himself, except this was republican politics with a dash of greyhound racing. Doors opened in Belfast and Buenos Aires: Miller was brought in, the wizard who made words on the page possible when Dublin believed nothing was more beautiful.

A book was born in three languages: the original Spanish text of Borges who had composed a map of Ireland that is not imaginary, for nothing is other than possible here; Englished by Kerrigan, Irished by O Suilleabhain, and bound by the Dolmen Press. It flew from the cuckoo's nest of Buenos Aires, to us. Nothing illustrates better why I preferred Kavanagh's bohemia to the other one. When Kavanagh visited my home town, he came as himself, with no idea of work in sight; he was there, he splurged, he rested, he went back. Borges could have imagined Miller and Kerrigan, the commendable rogue spark, he could not have invented the man from Mucker. To join Kavanagh was to be part of the aristocratic all day in the bar, ultimately justifying the verdict of May O'Flaherty in Parson's on Baggot Street bridge, "James Liddy is a nice man, but he has never done a day's work in his life."

An abode of Kavanagh's was Leland Bardwell's basement flat at 33 Lower Leeson Street. As the party came in after closing, Paddy was already asleep on the couch. He would not show any sign of life, except for the hand that went in and out under the pillow releasing and putting back the noggin of Scotch. He drank in his sleep. Once I was there with Liam O'Connor and Kavanagh woke up and was in tears. Everyone was in the pub, "I am dying, send out for the priest." We were close to a house of the Jesuits; we considered knocking on their door; but people started coming into the room, Paddy decided on resumption. Brown parcels were torn apart: life is all the days after opening day.

I drove Paddy from McDaid's many times: to different Leeson Street houses, to Upper Mount Street, to the South Circular Road. I drove him the last time to Amiens Street Railway Station in August 1967—just before I hit the San Francisco trail. He told me in the car everything was gone "except the liver." Kavanagh was probably as heterosexual as Baudelaire; the night Kavanagh died, as in Paris in 1867, the discussion was on among intimates as to whether he had left a virgin. I doubt that because he loved life despite his misgivings, he had purity that needed social expression, he had a partly comic passion for women; there was Katherine. I liked him, he was not ruined by a gift, I liked him, he was derisive. A favourite phrase was "very entertaining."

I lost sight of Kerrigan and find him only in 1990, just before his death. He's at Notre Dame, Indiana, a state and a bit away from me, going by Lake Michigan. Our Vergil is Frank Corcoran, Irish musician and professor, who meets him in South Bend and brings us together for the last letter:

> "I saw you at Liam Miller's in Mountrath. Willy-nilly your image has slipped into my daydreaming all

through the years since. I've often told the story of my laying of the wreath of your *Esau, My Kingdom for a Drink* on the then un-imaged tomb of the other James, in Zurich, as you asked me to do (and as I reported in Terence de Vere White's *Irish Times*). Two nights ago I gave a talk on Cela. I'll send pre-publication ms. (on Cela) from my Kellogg office when I return to North Siberia, U.S.A. On *The Family of Pascal Duarte* I'm earning big bucks (50% of royalties to me: best contract ever, so please order your orderly students to order, per carita.)

You once told me that your M.D. had told you to walk before breakfast. His advice cost me nothing. So I took it. And this P.S. is penned on return from the dawn (medio dia) paseo, to buy U.S.'s best and most tergiversational news-mongering paper, *The New York Times*."

You take your pick among the bohemians. There were other coteries besides these two—for instance, the indigent taxi squad around Brendan Behan, which careened to a screech outside McDaid's. This was a group which Jordan had difficulty in entering because of his allegiance to Kavanagh, and I could not join at all. With the present ideological lack of passion the Dublin post-bohemia has lost, as Austin Clarke might observe, "our intemperate habits." You can lead a horse to water and they drink—but must it be Perrier?

My era in Grafton Street labyrinths, which bought its rounds sometimes with naivete, seemed to gather for the last time when Paddy Kavanagh's widow Katherine died. The funeral, twenty two years after the poet died, brought the McDaid's tribe together. In the Church of the Three Patrons, Rathgar, the coffin was still in the side chapel while the monsignor robed on the altar. Three wispy altar boys rolled it along hitting the odd bench. Peter Fallon, in the pulpit, read the poem about Islington which Katherine told him was her favourite. The monsignor said life was a divine poem, streaked with light and darkness, it was like a Caravaggio painting the way the subjects are seen. Before the coffin moved down the aisle a woman sang "Raglan Road."

Outside, Miss King of the book shop bussed everyone. Across the street John Montague did business with an editor. Helen Moloney, Katherine's sister, went around asking if everyone had a lift. A turn around in Carrickmacross to get to the Dundalk road. The welcomes to Inniskeen, a picture of the poet, a sign for Shancoduff, the birthplace, the cemetery wall, a tall lad with an earring, "Where can I leave this wreath?"

The arts adviser to the taoiseach, Tony Cronin, conscripts poets to carry the coffin. Pass by the stepping stones to the poet's grave, past his sister Annie's—"Hope to see you all in paradise." The priest wears a hunting cap to the delight of an American student. Over the words of the resurrection, Helen Moloney's interruption, "No. No, I can't let this funeral go on, Katherine has stated her wish to be buried beside Paddy, it is in her will." Mary, the poet's sister, says, "Helen is right, she should lie with her own."

The solicitor goes down to the car for the will. He remarks, "The Atlantical wires must be buzzing." The priest decides there will be a delay of three hours while another grave is dug; the chairman of the Kavanagh Society gets up on a tombstone to reiterate the announcement. The mourners parade to the social club, the bar is open, pots of tea and sandwiches in the inside room. Ronnie Walsh says about the fuss, "Kavanagh would have loved it."

The poet's great nephew, John Lynch, drinks Lucozade and asks for a fag. Soon he is drinking black pints. His great grandparents lie inside the cemetery gates and no one bothers with them. "I'm glad I'm a Lynch, all the Kavanaghs are mad."

It's time. The crowd throngs out of the hall, up the road, up the side steps, back to the spot where the stepping stones with words have been removed. The hole is open. Mary looks into its openness, "This is Patrick's grave." She blesses herself with a piece of earth she takes from it. The poet is now old. The poets step forward to read a poem over Katherine's coffin down in the grave. Anthony Cronin reads "Bluebells." Michael Kane reads the poem about the watery hills. Leland Bardwell reads a poem of Pearse Hutchinson written to Katherine. I read, "Surely my god is feminine, for Heaven/is the generous impulse..." A local bard takes from his pocket a poem in which butterflies stray.

Katherine Kavanagh

I knew Paddy before I knew Katherine, the man before the woman, that must have been the Irish order then. Paddy was fond of referring to Listowel as "The Athens of the North," but he himself incorporated the famous daimon of the agora, akimbo and dangling; he was the architect's sketch of the poet; tall as a contemporary glasshouse and as strong as a horse. An incessant clamour against things as they are and people as they must be, a diatribe encased in gravel and buttressed in scotch, shook the market place of whiskeys and porters with beautiful savagery.

Paddy held court in McDaid's as tight as any Tudor. He also took Tudor advantages. The novelist John Broderick came in armed with white Switzer's shirts. Standing at the end of the bar he entreated, "Queue here for free shirts." Paddy jumped up and came back with three. Sean Dunne of the Labour party roared, "Get the nancy boy out of this."

Mainly there were melancholy receptions. A woman professor from the Carolinas had to buy him three brandies before he'd speak; he remarked, "I like Eich." "You like Ike?" she inquired. "I mean Eichmann." "Are you that eejit," he asked the Archbishop of Canterbury in Parson's bookshop. Archbishop Fisher's sin was that he had attacked on the B.B.C the wasteful expense of the space flight to the moon. The space adventurer side by side with the Mass-goer: the daimon surfaced. Paddy leaning in McDaid's door praising the heaven come to earth—he had seen the opening of the Vatican Council by Pope John on T.V. Or Paddy, at an English Literature Society meeting, avowing friendship for Archbishop McQuaid in the context of the latter's prohibition of attendance at the Yugoslav football match.

Paddy's romance of women was mysterious. He had courted with passion in his tea-room period, before the drink; he had the country regard for the urban milkmaid. Now there were attempted liaisons with medical students promising them trips to New York and Tiffany's (my sister was one of them, she never forgave me for giving away her address); he thought one day they would be rich. The other women around were mostly other men's wives, for as Tony Cronin observed of the pub entourage, "Paddy who used not like them is now surrounded by them." It was true: his court had expanded and grown more queer. Paddy's impression was only favourable in his crowd; Dublin expected but never liked the poet as ragged clever clerk, it much preferred the radical or the rebel, as it proved in its welcome for Michael Hartnett.

But Paddy went to London and stayed longer. Inevitably there stole across the Irish Sea the rumour of a woman. This became more and confirmed. Finally the poet was revealed as being in love, was Adonis and Romeo in the flesh, and was looked after and made happier. Soon Katherine, whom most already knew, would be coming over.

Katherine was in McDaid's coming over to me to give a little lecture on how to treat Paddy. She was apparently uncomfortable with Paddy's new friends from U.C.D. who had gypsy-gathered there. Gins rapidly in hand, she shone as the empress of the small bar and tiny lounge. Confirmed, she joined in every discussion; she was the sports and racing friend of most, specially of Paddy O'Brien, the head barman of McDaid's. Katharine really was the patria, in the core of its dreams, tastes, evasions, and secret glories, history sparkling in her face that seemed the same as her uncle Kevin Barry, the 18 year old medical student hanged by the British. I heard her voice later across the water, in the Museum bar, but I hesitated as I realised she was Gloriana with a bohemian London parked around her. The only Katherine I knelt to was Dublin's and Grafton Street's.

She was home for good. There was rumours, intense buzzing, Dr. Dickie Riordain convened about; finally my medical pal Tony Carroll told me the ultimate: the bans. In two days time the poet and Katherine would be joined in the church in whose choir James Joyce's father had met his mother. The ceremony was in progress when I arrived; twenty or so McDaid's folk watched as the nuptials were shuffled through despite outbursts from the husband-to-be. The cries of seeming dissent were probably only fractious comedy—at the "Do you take" stage I may have heard, "It has nothing to do with me." But what else does a man say? I heard afterwards that the bridegroom's friend, Archbishop McQuaid had instructed the officiating priest to ignore all side rumbles. Done, and when asked to go to the sacristy to sign the register the poet tossed his mane, "Bring the fucking thing here." (Later Katherine told me that when she visited the Kavanagh papers U.C.D. exhibition she saw in a case for the first time the Archbishop's letter of congratulation to Paddy and her.) Done, and soon the wedding party was streaming across Rathgar Road. The Evening Herald ran a photograph with the caption, "Bride and Bridegroom leaving church." It showed Dickie Riordain, car keys in hand, and Paddy Kavanagh approaching a vehicle.

The bride's house was nearby. Tony and I were introduced to her mother lying a-bed, an older version of Mise Éire. Tony's Tipperary neck of the woods appealed more to her than mine, though her sister Madame O'Rahilly broke in to say she had known my father well in college. The bridegroom wandered around until he was presented to Mac O'Rahilly.

Kavanagh got on to Mac's father's death in 1916, "That must have been a terrible end, dying drop of blood by drop of blood, lying there and no one coming to him for the snipers' cross-fire." The O'Rahilly paled beside Katherine's father who had been on hunger strike for 37 days in the Curragh. We all took off to Eoin and Joan Ryan's house, once owned by Joe Hone, the biographer of Yeats. Paddy couldn't eat the nuptial foods and an omelette was brought to the dining room table. We sat on the floor of the spacious drawing room while Paddy rendered "Lord Ullan's Daughter" and " Raglan Road" for us.

I met them one morning and went to their flat on Palmerston Road: how exhausted and down Paddy was while Katherine was cheerful. My sister met Paddy who chased her around the cake stand at Bewley's, gabbing about Katherine.

In San Francisco his death was in *The Chronicle*; I went down to Market Street to get *The New York Times*. Sure enough: the sub-heading ran, "Reputation for Eccentricity Said to Have Overshadowed Talents as a Writer."

In the summer Katherine was living in a basement flat on Fitzwilliam Place; she started working for her family in Chapelizod. She had our madness for sociability. She wanted to go driving on Sunday which was too reminiscent of my father. Now she was living in the kitchen basement of her father's house, we had to make no noise going upstairs to piss. Her sister Julie died crashing off the freeway to San Francisco airport on the way to collecting *The United Irishman*. On Katherine's bed lay the tricolour from Julie's funeral; I was often in that room drinking until the wee hours. One night Katherine presented me with the last shirt Paddy had worn (it was red), accompanied by a signed edition of a Kavanagh Press volume from New

York. I said, "At least Paddy's shirt is a different colour from Yeats's."

Then London, a Con Howard 'Paddy do' at the embassy. I spoke with John Hewitt, that mildly offensive man who tried to meter Kavanagh. In an Irish pub Katherine washed away my chagrin with her sympathy, "I know you didn't like it, pet."

Katherine decided to make her first and only visit to the States. She came to see me in Granville, Ohio, with a young friend, Carlos, an American about Dublin town. In one of my nasty fits, when the madness of the glasses were in us, I threw Carlos out when he made a speech praising the United States for what it had done for his family. Poor Carlos had to spend the night in his car. Katherine soon linked up with some hippies in one of my classes: she went out to stay at a farmhouse rented by Link Freeman and his friends.

To Newport with Hank Schlau in tow, that was when Thames Street was for sailors.

Jim's Place had a fight every five minutes; we felt Hart Crane stalking around—we stayed in a hotel over wind and water, three beds in the room, Katherine in one and me in Hank's bed with no result; lamentation and joy of drunkenness. Katherine liked the black cabmen we took here and in New York; she postponed the fare-paying by throwing her arms around them and talking about the struggle. We took a bus from Newport to New York passing through Harlem and went to stay at the Chelsea Hotel; we loved the cooker and the fridge in the room. We met Katherine's brother-in-law, Peter, for dinner in the Don Quixote next door. What Peter, in his autobiography, lays out as a plot by Katherine and her lawyer (I was an Irish barrister) to manipulate Paddy's estate was a continuation of our alcoholiers, just another lost luminous dinner. During the meal Peter went home and returned with signed copies of his books for us.

Katherine's father, James Moloney, died and Katherine never seemed to recover her poise—she had ailments of her own and slowly sank into an agitated, less self-reliant state. There were still excursions and occasions; journeys to friends in England, "Got card in Lavenham—tourist village of Suffolk. Off to annual visit to 'The Dell' (Elizabeth Smart). Ring me 19th. Hope your mother is OK." We went up to Inniskeen to see Paddy's grave; Katherine was not immediately pleased with Peter's poem-stepping stones to it. When I went back, she appeared in Grogan's to say goodbye; these were my American wakes of the late 70's/early 80's. Paddy O'Brien contributed a naggin of Irish to my journey, nature's old-fashioned gentleman. The last time Katherine was in Grogan's she complained about the cold and her friends despite Paddy's valiant attempts to get a sports conversation going.

Katherine could still come out. There was a Chinese place on Clarendon Street she liked; she told a good story, "At Mac O'Rahilly's funeral there was the Bar, the Judiciary, no politicians except Rory Brugha, a family friend. Some military men were saluting; Garret the silken Taoiseach was paying respects. Nobody seemed to be talking to him, I went up, "Thank you very much for coming." The Taoiseach replied, "The old Sinn Féin families should stick together." She liked the restaurant in the Rathmines town hall; she was miserable but did her best with a story, "I was canvassing for the Greens, I knocked on the door of the General Secretary of the Communist Party of Ireland; it was opened by Mrs. O'Riordain, "You are welcome, your late husband's friend toured the USSR with

Michael." The wife of the General Secretary did the correct thing, she produced a bottle of real Vodka. Around the corner Chaim Herzog, the President of Israel, was visiting his boyhood home. Over the cheers, Mrs. O'Riordain said, "We have a candidate, new to the Party, in the area, he won't win. Michael and I will give you our Number 2."

Katherine held soirées on Sundays. As I was in the country I could pick a weekday. She turned back to her civic republicanism and would go for my Blue Shirt ancestor. Once when I was in the bathroom she banged on the door crying, "Fascist, fascist." Her last story: It was the first day of Spring, the Feast of St. Brigid. Ever since she became ill she went to the nearest church; she didn't like the priests. It was the Church of the Three Patrons where she had been married. Bells in the distance; it must be the 9:30 Mass. A man stood at the doors, she asked him, "Is the 9:30 about to start?" "Oh, you're a bit late, the 9 has been going for awhile." She peeked inside to see if the spotlight was streaming on the tall statues of Brigid, Patrick, Colmcille. There was no light, she stumbled out, she shouted to the man on the footpath, "I'm never going back there again, I'm finished with those men."

Patrick and Katherine, we were unimportant as we deplaned at the unimportant airport.

Kavanagh in Glory

On a cold day in Evanston, Illinois, Patrick Kavanagh became a prophet as he stood in the academic temple and uttered blasphemous phrases. His pose on the occasion of a symposium on "Poetry after Yeats" reflected a typical stance: that the artist appears in society from under the boughs of the tree of life: "In fact I would say the only people in America that are alive are men like Jack Kerouac. *On the Road* is an excellent book, one of my favourite books about America since Henry Miller's *The Air-Conditioned Nightmare*, and I like Corso, Ferlinghetti, and Allen Ginsberg very much ... I have made it my bedside book for several years...." After sportive visits to the grand bookshop Hodges and Figgis on Dawson Street to buy another set of black and white City Lights books, I adjusted to the siren note of the Apocalypse carried by the Beat Generation. I knew the mainstream family had faded like the Fourth of July; it was time for experiments with literary form, poetics, the idea of performance, as well as with libido in general.

The Beats puttered around like us in the twilight zone. Kavanagh was attracted to the outré—in a letter to his brother he refers admiringly to that "rascal" Allen Ginsberg. Under McDaid's high ceiling we were in a San Francisco of our own union; in a duet between city and author, man and woman, or man and man, or woman and woman. Coincidently Kavanagh declared his preference for London, "They don't care who you are or who you're with, they don't ask questions, but mind you it is the same in ways as here, by the time you get to bed everyone is too drunk to take their clothes off." We imagined a Camelot of chandeliers and scotch. We lived every day (day and night) in an enchanted poetry harem of McDaid's.

We were caught in a global poetry house-warming. Brian Higgins reminisced for a drink, "George Barker was in the company, perhaps he had been let off the string, he certainly was in no hurry to leave the pub. 'Hey, George,' I shouted, 'have a drink.' 'Drop dead, filth,' was his reply, 'stop, stop, you're a beatnik.'"

So, in a way, was the condition of the bardic order after they were thrown out by the gate lodge to the bóthareen! They licked their wounds in public like Kavanagh and the Beats. There is an eerie quality of repetition here as evidenced by O Brudair's lines, "This vision in trembling death swoons ditched/clerks and poets, making them paranoid and hungry/lying in a rough bed, thinking of something terrible to say." For the Irish poets of the seventeenth and eighteenth centuries, for Kavanagh, for Kerouac and Ginsberg, authentic homelessness might be a description of a joint diaspora. Each have another alibi with the future, their poems or poem-like writings are bathed with the chemistry of patrons, barflies, local characters, and implicitly with rival poets.

The Irish Renaissance and the San Francisco Renaissance share elements of antinomianism; the force of Kavanagh's poems agree with the sense that, unlike the Gospels, the moral law is not binding, faith in the prayers and works of love is sufficient for salvation, love you study with (put into liturgy) casts out puritan fear. The Beat writers brought something special to this, a gift described by Leslie Fiedler as "the last, mad effervescence of the dreams of Utopian sex." The ideal of revolution against all revolutions, we ordered more pints as we didn't want to understand our world, we wanted to change it. We wanted to change ourselves into lovers, a thing never heard of in nationalist Ireland. The drinking hours were lengthened, weekends became festivals, the fleadh cheoils turned into Woodstocks.

The emphasis was on song, kiss, and your kind of dance. Edna O'Brien's first novels offered an alternative sensibility, they included women in the liberation rituals. My ancestral East Clare, and Brian Merriman, come to mind: the intuition that love and sex should be amusing to the point of being funny, but often aren't.

Patrick Kavanagh led us through the Eisenhower/de Valera decade. In his later work his poetics are like Kerouac's or Spicer's or Wieners's: flighty, not always muted, possibly spontaneous possibly innocent, the law of trying to stay with the first draft. The last five poems of *Collected Poems*, edited by me first in *Arena*, were a burning out of his previous sound, a coming out from the closet of a lifetime's masked sincerity. Kavanagh was and is Beat primarily because his lines are concrete and immediate. "Never after-think to improve," the best is "...the most painful, personal, rung-out, tossed-from-the-cradle, warm, protective mind." Tap yourself into the song of yourself. If with Yeats the elegiac heroics of Poe enters Irish literature via Mangan, then it is with Kitty Stobling that Whitman's "Song of Myself" lets loose in Dublin culture.

Mike Wallace asked Jack Kerouac, "This Beat Generation is a 'seeking generation' ... What are you looking for?" The response, "God, I want God to show me his face," strikes me as similar to Kavanagh's desire to find the same face in a cut-away bog. The muse of these writers' is fun and fantasy but is also driven by malice and satire. Kavanagh's poems are sheer textuality, the rendezvous description of experience, mimesis that the reader encounters on the pages of *Tristessa* or *Big Sur*. The sparkle of epiphany; if it sparkles, don't reheat it. Kerouac said, "I have to make my choice between all this and the rattling trucks on the American road. I think I'll chose the rattling trucks, where I don't have to explain everything, and where nothing is explained, only real." Kavanagh's advice is robust too, "Write about what is in front of you, write about that pint on the table." Kavanagh possessed the secret, he knew what to do to put yourself outside the establishment, "To be original and to have a comic attitude to life. What you would also want to say to put yourself outside is that Robert Graves and Marianne Moore are of no use." Use, that is the clincher, though give me Moore and not Graves. If anything, Kavanagh is darker, more negative, than the Beats.

Legend made the Beats stars like the sparkler liturgies that those of us who dwelt in McDaid's remember. Fame is a beautiful but devastating tune; my generation watched Kavanagh orchestrating that music, and we listened to those extraordinary songs coming from New York, San Francisco, Mexico City, Tangiers. Seduction is never a failure.

It all came back to me, on January 21 1982, in the Jazz Gallery in Riverwest, Milwaukee, when I meet Gregory Corso. "Paddy," he said, "was very sharp. Kavanagh knew he was a poet so he could sit with whom he liked. Oh, he was a good poet. Him and Brian Higgins, poor fuckers, they made a mistake, they bit the dust, but I'm alive. What a time we had in the Queen's Elm, going to the owner's house after hours. Those guys owned that man, I'm sure they never paid him, their credit was bigger than his bank account I'm sure."

And I sat down and wrote to Paddy's widow and my friend, Katherine, in Rathgar what Corso had said, until he was taken off to the snake pit by my students. "Holy Barbarians," instruct us from where you are, the starry heavens your beds.

Liam Miller and *The Dolmen Miscellany*

This volume came on the scene in the midst of a heyday for a coherent band of writers, the first group since Yeats and The Renaissance. Liam Miller designed the brooding, dark red edge of its cover which, halfway between a journal and an anthology, heightened the effect of a coup. Its vinuous appearance gives the atmosphere of the haunts it was conceived in. We were on a blazing trail with sorties of Roethke and Berryman though our doors, with the expatriate pomp of Edward Dahlberg's elegant yarns over a Leeson Street shop, or Richard Ellman in Miller's company paying his bill at the Shelbourne Hotel with a cheque printed in Gaelic, or Sylvia Beach and Maria Jolas on deck chairs by a just opened Sandymount tower, aloof from milling glasses.

The Miscellany represented the climax of the first stage of the Dolmen Press with the emphasis on the publication of local poems; once Miller had set up a nucleus of arresting poets he turned his attention to the lucrative? Elysian meadows of the U.S. campus. Scholars came and went to the Baggot Street office like Lady Gregory's swallows. How Miller, in front of his bookcase of William Morris, Harry Clarke, and Eric Gill, awaited the call of the academic airport bird; the first in line got Mrs. Yeats—the others fashioned out over the rich post-"leprechaun or garrulous rebel" terrain.

The Miscellany is a manifesto by sample and by editorial. The guerilla preface still seems warm, its tartness a call to exterminate the bucklepper, its "...a little solemnity may be a revolutionary gesture" a Baudelaire provocation (1962 leading back to 1857). This is Montague's call to arms; it is Parisian: to the barricades! Odd as it may seem,

McDaid's was the clearing house to which we fled from *The Bell* realists and the desk-bound Coole twilight. There, over the counter or at the few tables, we summoned the country's muses and its engineers.

Miller was a sort of Celtic Diaghilev, both for design flair and total networking. Breathtaking, he did the funding dance. There was touch of the four Yeatses about Miller and he dearly loved them: he built the magisterium of an august press name together with a basement image of an arts and crafts operation; a presentation of mother Eire filtered into the golden, indeterminate performance of post-liberation. Liam had specifically a link with W.B.— both pragmatic and theoretical inclinations in regards to the theatre and some dissimilarities: the replacement of Rosicrucianism with Romanism, the occult by the tavern.

Liam Miller accomplished a new phase in Irish poetry without in any way caring to write it. Critics talk of the dominance of the Cuala and Dolmen presses but there are quite a few exceptions.

For instance, Dolmen had little to do with an interest in Kavanagh; but I stood on Baggot Street bridge while Miller photographed the Monaghan poet for *Self-Portrait*, the printing of a R.T.E. essay, the sole Dolmen publication of a Kavanagh work. His influence is all through the Miscellany; his aura floats on the poems including mine and is most visible in the contributions of John Jordan. McDaid's is the scene of Jordan's story "First Draft."

What was it that induced our nonpareil begetter to march us off to the United States, past the Blaskets and the Arans to the cocktail cabinet? Perhaps a biography of Miller would be too complex a task to allow us have, even in time, extensive answers to such queries.

Liam Miller and I acquired many pub flier-miles, astonishing conversations. I remember a few: both of us with Donagh MacDonagh, a small man, and his wife Nuala in Neary's. Theodore Roethke appears shining with wear and makes for Nuala who tries to introduce him to Donagh. "You're married to that gargoyle?" Roethke was incredulous.

I remember Miller at Yeats's Corcomroe Abbey with Mary Holland—we were asked in the hushed tones of Synge to leave the pub because the owners were going to a funeral. Another funeral, that of Louis MacNeice in Belfast with Liam and Tom Kinsella; afterwards making our weaving way through groups of MacNeice's friends in houses and pubs—I had not understood how vast the liberal pre-WWII Protestant community had been there. Also how after a "tiring day in the field" Liam would bring me back to a wonderful spontaneous omelette in his kitchen. Downstairs his office awaited, or rather the office-drawing room of illustrated and fine art books. Liam would take down a Gill and expound it with a seraphic, enigmatic, smile. He made beautiful pages of his own on those never-ending summers. Baggot Street was never deserta in those days.

Michael Hartnett Through My Dark Glass

In the sixties it happened again, a countryside opened to showcase a poet. Townlands spoke. Like Kavanagh, came out of the earth unstoppable. Whatever spotlighted these country lads riding wild horses, bards of a rural Hollywood, violently beautiful (Stephen Spender said to Kavanagh in *The Encounter* office, "Your poems are violently beautiful"). Kavanagh better on points than Hartnett because he played the violin more slackly from horseback, riding winners their common lot. Where did it come from: out of a god that is not exactly Bacchus nor Dionysus (though these two introduced themselves), perhaps from the sound of a neo-god the player of music first in fields and then in public houses, staves for throats divine and dry.

Paul Durcan showed us a photograph of the "teaboy" of the western world, Michael working at the tea break in an English factory. Jordan and I investigated and arrived in Newcastle West. That kitchen we found through Bishop street ("without a bishop") Maiden street ("without a maiden"), in 28 Assumpta Park. Younger brothers playing football outside, Dennis the father already gone out and going out again. We went with him, we heard song and some fables of the West Limerick Labour Party.

Thereafter we ushered Michael into McDaid's golden cave where he was given the treatment, coaxed, appraised. He walked around the firing squad. John, ascetic Dean of Letters, gave him a pound a week for a year and talked of supporting him through First Arts at U.C.D. I contributed the day to day pint money of salvation. Dinny O'Dwyer, Paddy Kavanagh's aide de camp, seemed to approve of him. Hartnett had his first caper at the party to launch *Poetry Ireland* in the Bailey, Ben Kiely in braces, Liam

Miller leading the chorus, downstairs Richard Murphy in whisper-mutter with Ted Hughes and Sylvia Plath.

Michael settled in through the poet-laden lanes of the never ghost-deserted city. He began to acquire what he termed "artistic temperament." Kavanagh swore by the magic of the opening of the Second Vatican Council; but Michael said, "I don't like the Pope." "Why not?" "I don't like his clothes." Michael wrote this period up in an unpublished novel; he did publish an account of a visit, with John, me, and a bottle of sweet sherry, to Austin Clarke's in Templeogue.

The sixties consisted of grand tours between various "raths." We were often in Kilkee; Michael liked Scott's pub, there was a small window in the back where he could watch the Atlantic breakers. Once when he and MacDara Woods were staying in my mother's house there, they answered a knock at the door armed to the teeth with colonial spears (which mother had bought at an auction at Clonderlaw). I remembered his hunger, how he ate all the butter on the table in the Glentworth Hotel.

We become figures in a mist. I thought of him on the Feast of the Epiphany because he was one of the Magi. In September, 1967, I left for San Francisco via Heathrow, I stayed overnight in London in his and Rosemary's house. Soon, he was back in Dublin working at the international telephone exchange; sometimes his voice raised in song lifted my ear in the U.S. I saw him summers in Grogan's.

I met him in the Aosdána meeting in Kiltimagh. Lively in the bar he remarked, "James, I owe you money," and gave a wad into my hand. A minute later laughing he grabbed it back. I knew our people always wrote poetry, star-fed, star-mad in March. Michael drank out of the skulls of bards from more places than Kerry.

I met him at the top of Grafton Street distributing a letter Allen Ginsberg had written him from the Temple Bar Hotel at 4 a.m. It was full of technical praise for his verse. He had made a 100 copies for the passersby.

He told a good story. Pat rang up early one morning, at the time when Quinnsworth were giving free oranges with South African wine. Pat and Richard were quarrelling; Michael went over to help, Pat let him in, there were oranges on all the chairs, the couch, as Michael took a glass.

Today in my mind I am meeting him somewhere, maybe on the border of Limerick city and county. Michael Hartnett closes the door and walks out to the star-wide field, unbuttons his shirt and eats the mushrooms and the dew in the morning. He told Nuala Ní Dhomhnaill he blamed his ill-health on Natasha. "Natasha who?" "Natasha Smirnoff."

Michael on the way out all summer. What a way for a bard to go out, on the phone! Calls to the house at Coolgreany, a call while I was in O'Neill's, a call to Milwaukee a month before he died. He said Angela was away for the weekend and his daughter had brought him over lunch: an orange, a bottle of vodka. He sang a stave on Inchicore and recited a poem written for me, a carrot on a vegetable stand gets up, walks across the road, and is crushed by a van. Goodbyes must be recited as well as sung.

Bog fairy country accent, lilting, looking like a changeling, famished, dry, unstoppable, bemused, telling the same story to the people at the next table. There is a priest in us, a Jacobite in us, maybe a gunman in us. From the day in the kitchen to the day in the hospital he had ancestors: Raifteiri and O Brudair, two pouters. Wine in remembrance. There is love, there is literature, music under stars at the crosswords, the zone of words floor-swept, sated, and sand-blasted.

With Michael Hartnett in Spain and Morocco 1964

The "t" had not yet come into "Harnett," there was still a not quite defined volatility, the countryman was there but the countryman in the city had not consolidated. There was now a turning to the Mediterranean, to the gods and goddesses of its amphitheatres and city walk-arounds, the wine and garlic lanes, and across the British-monkey-watched sea to the fez and turban in 20th century glitter and French Deco spas (just being vacated). A gorgeous curtain was going up on new Bohemian artmaking, twisting in the Beat music from the clubs of the United States, and we wanted to balance it with a Graeco-Roman basis. Then Michael could return to the McDaid promenade and rest areas of Co. Limerick, and I to the similar swan-singing around Kavanagh and convalescences of Co. Wexford.

Michael, Barry Cusack, and I arrived in Malaga airport and shortly afterwards found ourselves in a basement bodega with young white-aproned guardians of the wine. Each order was on the slate, and at the end of a stretched evening we offered to pay but no one knew the amount. A gracious introduction to the land of Francisco Franco, Lorca's singing ghost, and Philip II's gout-chair. Next morning a tram to the beach but we had no time to contemplate a swim: a row of bar-restaurants knelt invitingly on the sand with fresh fish cooking. Talking is a reflection of landscape and we were instantly lyrical, Barry drooping behind us. Next morning we were in La Linea, up on the roof of our hotel we saw and knew the Moorish world with the crickets' sound. So Lorca was in the continuing line of these ghosts.

I got a swim on the beach next to the rock of Gibraltar, Michael guarding the heap of my possessions; we leant away from the monkeys and did not cross over into that portion of empire. We went instead to the ferry and saw the blue hills of Africa looming up. Michael started talking about Hemingway. Our guide kidnapped us on landing though we had the name of a French hotel in the casbah. At the registration desk Americans were asking where Paul Bowles lived. Sitting in the Socco Chico *Interzone* passed in its charming and furtive costumes. I made us go to the French section to look for Tennessee Williams. In the morning, Ahmed was in our bedroom patiently waiting for his gentlemen to wake up and moan their hangovers. He told us about girls and boys, the latter cost twice as much because it was not as right. Michael asked him about keif, that was not good either. He took us to the party of our lives on Tangier beach. All night at one end we kept sending for beer as three musketeers entertained us, they seemed to live in a space under the sand. They said they were in Franco's Foreign Legion, they saluted the Spanish flag with a fascist hymn: our face to the sun. Their concluding act was to go down their hole, then come up in women's clothes and wiggle for us. The next night we went to a club and young Arab girls danced, at least Barry and Michael thought they were girls!

We headed for Chauen up in the mountains, James Crosbie had told me about it in McDaid's. Michael must have got some keif somewhere; our bus was stopped by the police, and Michael in agitation let some fall. It spilled across the floor but the officials were not interested in tourists. We put up in a Berber hotel and explored. I walked up the hills and lay down under an ilex tree; camels passed. Michael went wandering to the new hotel on the town's edge, and spied a car with Irish number plates; he was revolted. The Spanish had just left, Spaniards were running empty cafes. We bought drinks for youngsters because they were not bound by the Koran.

They said their families had keys to houses in Granada. Back in the hotel room, Michael read Neruda.

We were discovering Morocco was more expensive than Spain, so back on the ferry. Lovely fish soup brought by old Algeciras waiters. Return to the caverns of Andalucia.

3

Glimpses of the Ramstown Arts Festival

Radio Ramstown

"The Arts Fest in this town has put Ramstown on the cultural map of Ireland, indeed on the cultural map of Europe." Jon Higgins, Director General of RTÉ, speaks after the address of the Minister, in the Art Centre. "It has brought to this part of the country an appreciation of a whole spectrum of artistic activities, from the plastic arts of painting and sculpture to the performing arts of music and drama. This is not a fringe event."

A man is speaking, not a television set, but still Homo Televisionus.

"Great credit is due to the Director of the Fest, and to the small band of helpers who have been bitten by the MacFaustus bug."

So—Television man has heard of the new dance!

The Fest clique, the non-guard of the legion, the Ramstown Rotters—Seamus, William, Aidan, maybe Lawrence—presbyters in the willows, croakers in the grass, feel like going up on stage to do the dancing man with fake Oscars in their hands.

"The one fest development I can personally lay claim to is Community Radio. Community Radio is a unique service, I remember when I came first some years ago here there was a sort of wired broadcasting service operating from loudspeakers on the streets during Fest Week."

(We remember: "Today is 'Round the Houses Relay Race.' It starts after tea at 7.30. Folks, have your tea on time. The race will start and finish at the Market House and the route will be the Avenue, Railway Road, and on to Main Street. There has been a revival of the pastime of skittles and matches are taking place nightly at North Parade—this is for new and old timers.")

The Director of RTÉ warns against local radio taking the form of a number of pop stations which in no way can be a service for the community. He is equally adamant against the money generated by local radio being siphoned off to private shareholders. Profits must go into broadcasting for the whole community. When he concludes his remarks, the Director of the Fest, Sean MacFaustus, presents Mrs. May Higgins with a bouquet of flowers and makes a further presentation, on behalf of the Fest committee and "The International Year of the Child," to Mrs. Higgins's six weeks old baby, Anthony Garrett.

The Fest starts, its radio is fluttering.

Radio Ramstown goes on the air and stays on it for a week, over a radius of 15 miles. Broadcasting 2.2 metres long wave and on 96.6 on UHF/FM.

The Fest Administrator, also the Entertainment Manager, speaks each morning detailing main events and fringe events of the day. Sean MacFaustus contributes later in the morning a six part serial—a nostalgic look at the idea of fests through the ages and in pre-Christian Ireland. It sets up a talent search for an announcer to be called Leinster Hermes who would make quick glad eyes like silver at the public.

MacFaustus worries if the program textures are plush enough, if they combine enough velvet and leather for youth.

The station is housed in the mobile unit parked outside the corrugated iron gates of the Fest Centre. Social life moves into the van, beer, sausage and chips or fish and chips. Debate that ends in a tender embrace before it is time to go on the air. Just before it begins broadcasting it turns into a real radio station.

Radio Lust hooks up to the gods and the unconscious.

Radio Turn Up, Radio Turn On.

Radio Cuckooland, Radio Cuckold, Radio Fest for Fest's sake.

It has its patter. "The consistent fluency of the 'sean Teanga' is as confusing as ar son na dTeanga, no, ar son na banga." At breakfast it distinguishes between the old cadhain and the new caidhean. At lunch time the program is "Sure What's the Differ?" and at night music is provided by courtesy of "The After Twelve Consort." "What you can't see in the dark sees you," ah, After Midnighters, Earring of Ivory, Dive of Gold, Mystical Pose, Boys of the Radio Band.

Each night before it pulls down the verbal curtains it utters in the Celtic tradition an astonishing and wise proverb. On the last Saturday, closing herself down, it proclaims through the exhausted chuckle of MacFaustus, "Better not count your chickens before they's hatched, old Brazilian 'sean-fuckle.'

Collect your dance partners now."

Politics

The Director thought he could get more from the Philosophers-Fixers than from the Foxrock Princes. He liked the Republican root and branch of the countryside, as a child he remembered Fr. Sweetman's funeral passing the house, he who had preferred Tara to Rome.

He wouldn't listen to Seamus who said in his cups, "Parnell was a gentleman, he died well in advance of 1916."

He gambled with drying up his art; soon he was wheeling, dealing, gesticulating sideways, whispering in ear after ear, putting out cigarettes, dropping ash, berating churls. The groans of politics are heard on the mountain top of vodkas. He was under Government, Arts Club spotlight. Each Mafia Midas had to give him the golden touch. He didn't live in a wand loft anymore—he rushed from lead tavern to silver tavern.

He looks now for those who "carry" the nation in their pockets.

MacFaustus is under surveillance, he is watched to establish if he has more perceptions than men of recent property. He is cross-examined silently as to the source of his peculiar traits. They fear the absence of a townland in him. He plays along with them, flaming in golden cups, through Courtless licences, Robert Emmet fairy fixerland, green grass on this shore of the sea in foam.

They have power and offshore cash, he wants fame and funding, the theatre of entitlements.

Their banshee de Valera combs his dark New York hair.

Sits on Howth Head or the Rock of Cashel, does it matter? MacFaustus winces, is star-struck. He runs back for soul's sake to the fun and solar society of the dancing men of the Fest (the logo of the Fest is the dancing man).

Drunk as a punk, yet he prays daily to Nijinsky, avatar of dance, custodian of Czarist beauty.

Nijinsky at least was never in Ireland, unlike his co-planet dancer Rimbaud who was in Cork for 24 hours, between ships.

Most of the time the Director dances with numbers, alas box office figures. The voice of his administrator, "Man, it's no dancing matter," rises. The Bank Manager wants more sherry at the reception. MacFaustus tries to talk to the state arts agency which has politicians trapped inside its body. The state must be gold dust: thou art gold and unto thine heirs gold will return!

Will they give us a loan of one of their collars of gold?

The future, not a future, doesn't quite understand its dance steps. Its Art is enough for them, but he imagines he hears softer voices of the grasses clinking their dews. Stalks of destiny. Stack them up.

Carlos di Medici, come to us.

The American Poet at the Fest

The sirens have had to suffer only a slight sex change, a small cold in the system, to transform their songs. Then they sing like tenors with a slight lisp. The poet has to step in and out of this stream. A better wet of his clothes.

Sean MacFaustus, painter, impresario, understands the mystery. He tries to keep some hot Fest seats for the poets. The warming of the Fest is in progress. Poets fly in on sirens' wings. By phone MacFaustus had contacted a dozen great poets. His mission, for all parts of his art empire, was to speed up madness and convert it into performance. A great poet has to be coaxed and dragged, specially from the one free sexual country in the world; the Barbary shores of new world coasts. This great poet originated from a large farm upstate New York or from the middle-class ghosts of a farm, by way of a couple of great universities, a poet with bucolic fame. Perish the flesh, MacFaustus gambled, on the day it does not proceed to its seed game.

Jim Ashman and his secretary Ben Bone were sent Aer Lingus tickets in Manhattan. Ashman was proclaimed on Fest posters and on local radio/television. The photograph used was thin, chic, camp, charming. Mr. New York/Ms. American Academy of poets was going to be in town— poetry was swingin' and swingin' was poetry.

That lack of inner peace that is the signal of first-rate intelligence! The clock of the flesh goes forward to midnight. The great poet hovers over Shannon airport waiting for the fairy fog to lift from the runway.

MacFaustus pants away to the early morning crowd, "Ashman is coming, Fest is going bankrupt, this is the last one, we're dribbling away, this is the big bang to wake up the bog that will survive us. When I phoned Ashman, I told him the delay in arrangements was due to the fact that we were a banana republic—we are an art oasis in a banana republic, but the package is together. I think he got a little tired of me in his Bloody Mary afternoon." Kevin and Ned were with MacFaustus; Kevin's wife had left for bed. Ned, a safe man, leaves for his house and wife. Kevin whispers, "Sean, I want to go to bed with you, I've wanted to for years." "But, Kev, you are always surrounded by girls, they've been going in and out your door by the new time. You could knock me over with a feather, if only I'd known." They go into MacFaustus's house, like two pupils coming from a playground going to their supper. They lie down and burst against each other, "I never knew how to approach you ... there are thousands waiting out there for you." They light cigarettes, Fest mood is set.

They are waiting by the maestro as he airport-gleams. Ashman has been giving a reading in London, following Auden's ghost slippers. Shy, exhausted, he tells them his first story, "At the reading an Indian student came up to talk to me, he said he was from Lucknow. I opened two buttons on his shirt and said, 'Look now, pay later.'"

Ashman is as slight as Joyce with a resemblance to him, and just as loaded. But kind and full of mirth, Ashman is the sweetest Jezebel. Technically it begins badly, he asks the barman, "Have you Boodles?" "Never heard of that one, Sir." "Well, then, I'd like a Bombay." "Never heard of her, Sir." "Then where is our friend the martini? It's not very Ritzy here is it?" Ben, to mollify, talks a little, "We went to a gallery, the local ashcan art. The main conversational remark Jim made in London was, 'It's five hours earlier in New York.'"

In the car Ashman looks out at Ireland tears in his eyes, "It's sad here, I see Frank's face everywhere. God, was he a bitch on the second day of a drunk."

The Dean at Harvard expelled one of his friends for the usual reason. "My friend asked the Dean, 'What year is it' '1949 of course.' 'No, it's not, it's 1492 and you know it.' I asked Auden for a recommendation for the Guggenheim, I saw him shortly afterwards at a party and asked had he done it? Wystan said, 'You do push a girl don't you.'" MacFaustus remembered what Seamus told him, "Paddy Kavanagh said, 'Only queers call him Wystan.'" Ensconced in the ice cream parlour, Ashman relaxes more, "The first sentence I remember is: vote for Hoover, save the country." Later Ashman startles everyone, "I have nostalgia for Nixon." He looks around, he was going to ask where he was—then he remembers. "I like Dublin. Dublin is a road show version of London. So this is MacFaustus City."

It spread before us like Babylon in its great outrageousness. Jim and Ben, action, poppers everywhere. Sober moments being interviewed by *The Irish Times*, the huge reading on Fest stage; Dionysian mementoes; a pub routine, "Who is that gorgeous hunk over there?" "That is the captain of the Ramstown Rugby club." "And that gorgeous hunk?" "Another member of the club." "I guess it's my game." Seamus's house in a village is the scene of the Fest garden party; Ashman sees on the table by the tennis court a bottle of rum, he sees two American priests, he crawls over the grass towards them, "I want to be received into the Catholic Church." They're not working. "How is it every time I ask to get into the Catholic Church it backs away." He is led upstairs for a rest. In a while Seamus and MacFaustus are summoned from O'Rafferty's next door, the women in the house hear noises. A strange man?

We say farewell to the American poet at 4 a.m. He is lying in the gutter outside the Railway Hotel smoking one of his fat hashish cigarettes in the headlights of a squad car.

An American in The Inn

The barman is ducking in amongst the bottles, "I'll fix you up, Mr. Mac ... I'll be with you in a second ..." all the time running up and down the stairs. Suddenly there is an American lady, she is a lady because she doesn't drink. Instead she says, "I think Mickey Mouse has destroyed the imagination of the American child." A drunk in the jakes calls out, "Micky Mouse is a rat."

MacFaustus attends her, the rustle of a check? "I went down to Westport to see if they'd house the painting collection of Earnie's. The Urban Council took me on a tour, telling me what they would do, they want to put them beside the bacon factory. Yes, my husband was a friend of Hart Crane, he was published in *Poetry Magazine*. My husband was a red-headed man when I met him in a New York bar." MacFaustus pulls up against her in a local whisper, "I know the scene, I am an Irish artist, and I have worked with the Arts Council. The only chance you have."

The barman continues to pour drink into everyone except the lady. The lady says, "Prices in Ireland are impossible." She has kept the taxi waiting two hours outside, before she goes back to Dublin she buys herself and the taximan fish and chips, which they eat on the seats.

Two off duty Gardaí have been sitting watching, drinking pints of Guinness and eating ham sandwiches. One of them, very red-faced, turns to the other and says, "I'll get you, you don't know where Nishapur is and what it's famous for?" "Mother of Jesus, I wouldn't know to save my own life." "I'll tell you now. It's the place where Omar Khayyam was born."

Farmboy at The Fest

Ben Bone is drunk. I take him to see mother who puts out the silver, the wine, and the salmon. She doesn't understand though. They are so polite to each other, and run out of conversation. Ben says, "I'm only an old queer from New York." "Ben," I say, "remember you're a farmboy from Missouri, mother is from Far Rockaway." Later he howls in the Ice Cream lounge, "Chick, not chicken.... I have no friends, nobody wants to kiss me, my only friend is Ashman who will get me jobs and positions."

MacFaustus is going to rent a car so Ben can drive the visiting poet around. "I must call Larry Rivers again to see if he'll come. He's hard to communicate with, must be on something."

Fest passes like a longer dream anecdote. Ashman and Ben on poppers and whiskey, MacFaustus on pills and vodka, me on vodka and stout. Sic transit gloria civitatis.

Walks in convoy, with some girls, through the Courtown woods to build sand castles with bedrooms in them on the Beach. Improbable never ending, maybe groping, night in the Railway Hotel which serves the drinks for the end of the world. Kisses, nobody knows where they start and end.

Ben and Ashman are saying farewell. Ben and Ashman on the last morning repair to the Ice Cream lounge: libations, to travel libations. Ashman puts his arm around Colm Tóibín and Ben—shakes hands with the rest of us. His shirt is, as usual, open, sirenising. "I like the Fest, I want to come back, can I come back? It was nice here after London, more like an 18th century town, like London used to be.

Ou est Monsieur MacFaustus, ou est mon check?"

Ashman is eternal speaker, Harvard–Paris, not Hollywood–
Beijing. Pulchra ut luna, beautiful as the moon when it is
empty. East Coast moonscapes, Paris steeped in arses,
some beautiful.

Manhattan is a fairy ring around Upstate.

Ben is not Hollywood, a cowboy among cowboys; he is a
farmboy among Wexford farmboys.

Mother at the Fest

The Railway Hotel is crammed with Fine Gael T.D.s, doctors in beach house slacks, beautiful poet boys, beautiful Brontë girls, and would-be Greeks. Aidan a-gleam with Brenda the Co. Clare mermaid; brother David with a little blond. Mother stayed through the play, 'The Yellow Bird,' Yeats and Maud Gonne in their cages tangling; no tango.

David salutes mother, gets up, buys, and pours for her a brandy and ginger ale. He kneels at her feet and then introduces her to his sisters, who kneel at her feet.

Mother has her story to tell, about theatre long ago. It's about a friend, James Gilvarry, later famous Joyceanna collector.

"He bought Chinese vases, Joyce letters, knew Izzy Cohen's shop when he was 15. James went back to America at the beginning of the war, his basement flat in Merrion Square was chock-a-block with books and antiques. His sister and I didn't know what to do." I reply, "He must have been a Cocteau invention." David, his sisters, are mused. Mother has the floor despite the milling. "James and I used to go to plays, specially George Bernard Shaw's. We sat through the two nights of *Back to Methuselah*. He'd be over to me from where he lived on Hampstead Heath, your father would come home from the hospital to be jealous. Once you were terrible as usual, pushing and shoving me around, and James said, 'Clare, you're just like a doll playing with a baby.'"

What can I say, "What Thirties ambience." David buys mother another Remy Martin and finalises, "And now the atmosphere of Fest town."

MacFaustus arrives, still madly lowering the Moussey. Almost red in the face, he has got a call from Pablito, "He's blowing hot and cold." Karl has phoned from Dublin, he has lost the key of MacFaustus's apartment, "I think he wanted me to go up to him in a helicopter." The Director jogs into another circle of Fest Inferno.

I sit by mother, thinking how beautiful and implacable the womb remains, there is nowhere else to go for one half of your life.

4
America

Elegy for Professor Dunleavy

Days of our lives, Janet ...

Wall Street's foundations fled
the Kennys were selling books to UWM,
we passed Chris Foley crying out his eyes
"I will never get into medical school now."
Gareth at home with a bottle of whiskey,
"I've lost hundreds of thousands—drink,"
my pure mind rose to Connaught's princes
and princesses, to Miss O'Conor of Clonalis,
"My father told me, 'remember you're the princess
of Connaught.'" (O Cassandra of the West,
I walked backwards before you that day).
The O'Conor Dun's papers rustled like a pack of dance cards
as Gareth and Janet indexed them
though no dancing down the long hall—
it is cold in Roscommon, Janet, the rain folds
on images, raths and hazel trees
outside railway carriage windows:
Roethke in a straight jacket
in Ballinasloe whose eyes shine like islands—
I ponder you in the Aras na nGael club
you are served if you speak in Irish,
you would be served. Tall drunk dances
to bodhrán as if he is a woman,
"I'm the worst dancer on Ireland ... I love women ...
I've lost my woman," and never is dancing so gay;
small man with a sailor's cap, a half-salute,
"Tá siar níos fearr ná soir,"
"West is better than East,"
(ag dul soir go Beal Átha na Sluagh)—
some Catholic mansions burnt some not
on Lough Carra the mist

but no thrall of princes:
George Moore, you were a dandy in Galway
an heir of Mayo; you, Janet, the chatelaine
over blackened walls fallen-in fireplace
clumps of grass in chimneys. At Miss O'Conor's
table you blessed yourself in the name
of the father the son the holy ghost ...
stunned yourself .... You are third person now.

Much is professor and book
much David Greene NYU The Arans the Book of the People,
much the look of the dead windows over the lake,
petroled Moore Hall—it is not enough.
Death stands here the bard-reaper no other
frogmarcher of gentry and grove.
She helped you or she didn't
help you at all.
That is more than most do.
Live in certain hearts.

The Year of Love, San Francisco

I say goodbye to mother, father, Nora, Liam, Paddy, Miriam, MacDara and the rest. With the exception of the first three we are flower-children, at this moment tear-struck.

I enter the new world flying the polar route. An Australian sits beside me, repeating how great his country is. I am going, I say, to a place about which I have only a literary idea. I go slowly through immigration at Los Angeles and fly up to San Francisco. From the airport bus I stare out the window at the Beat streets. In the Beresford Hotel I unpack a little, ten p.m., the hour of sorties. Joe Gardiner, great Coolgreany publican, had recommended Harrington's at Jones and Market; he told me you have to say yes immediately in the U.S. if someone invites you to a drink. No Irish coaxing! This is the most valuable piece of advice I got.

On the first corner I stand, a pioneer before the lights of Captain Bligh's Bounty. I sail into my first bar. Along the counter a mature white man sits on a bar stool, a younger black man beside him, this is repeated down the bar. The last slot is vacant, I order my first across-the-ocean beer. What will be my fate?

Around the next corner the lights say, Harrington's; a big place. In the foyer reigns a signed photograph of Bobby Kennedy. A chieftain. An old man is moving the fiddle, I am asked the usual details on place and family. I prove myself a Milesian. The Irish Rovers play in the gallery. I realise I am the age of someone, 33.

The telephone lines crackle in the Beresford next morning. An old Limerick accent remembered my grandfather,

Daniel Liddy, farmer and butcher, walking up the railway tracks at Kishiquirk to Mass. The next voice says Mary Conlin, a first cousin of my best medical pal Anthony Carroll—like to see Monterey and Big Sur? We drive in her sports car along the coast. Among the sights: a red-faced monsignor at a mission looking as if he is eating his breviary, a Canary Row bookshop where I buy George Moore in exile homage, Robinson Jeffers's house in what seems a sour beach glow. I see my first snake, shades of St. Patrick, and gulp my first screwdrivers at Nepenthe; the cliff house Orson Welles bought for Rita Hayworth as a wedding present. I piss against my first redwood tree. In this fashion I set myself to conquer California.

Frisco, brilliant, seducing, a breezy cauldron; I feel surprisingly "in." Everyone good humoured, travellers checks cashed in a second. Spanish architecture, Spanish radio, this is a second Dublin for me, like Palma. Flower children in profusion, but people say the scene is moving out to rural parts.

To the campus of San Francisco State, just a few acres. Rebellion brews. Someone tells me there is an area reserved for dope-smoking behind the cafeteria, a nude-in is taking place on the lawn. Helen Pettit in the English Department hands me a key to my office down the corridor from Business professors. I have a neighbour at the other desk who introduces himself as Nic Kubly. He tells me he is a writer from Wisconsin who has received the National Book Award for non-fiction. He invites me for cocktails to his house in Waller Street. By the time I arrive from downtown into Haight Ashbury's dreamland he has talked to the English-born owner next door and I have a basement flat. It is a condemned habitation and I want to be a condemned writer. I whoopee into the night because I have landed at last.

You go around to the back of the house which dates from 1870 and up some rickety steps to a big front room. A sink with hot water, presses, fridge, gas cooker, a table, a couch I have made out of two mattresses with the help of a yellow blanket. The second room is almost as big, bed, wardrobe, pigeon-hole Victorian desk. Then a shower. My house, half a mile from Golden Gate Park, for $65 a month, including electricity and gas. I celebrate by walking up Haight Street. A bearded man has a reefer and waves it in front of a crowd who are down on their knees begging for a smoke.

Nic Kubly drops by, but usually stays for only three drinks. He expects me to visit him for a cocktail at the happy hour. From his window you can see the Bay Bridge and Oakland. He is writing his big Greek book which is a mixture of fact and fiction. Knowing all Irish people are expert professors of history, he inquires about Elizabeth of Austria-Hungary, "Sissi." He is on the Corfu section and he has her in the palace with her maid combing her hair and suddenly the beautiful woman shrieks—one hair is grey. Kubly is what I've admired, an intimate teller of tales. He is in conflict with Joyce-confidant Kay Boyle; she got him the job at State and wanted him to live in her house on Frederick Street and when he refused an academic war ensued. Another creative writing colleague, Bill Wiegand, tells me, "We don't give tenure to journalists." That's the Time/Life label against Nic who was music critic of the first, did the Italy book for the second.

Nic has brought back, from his last time in Greece, a boy who is being educated near the farm in Wisconsin; he will appear at Christmas and I will meet him. At the urging of Wisconsin senators, Nelson and Proxmire, Alex has been made a citizen by an act of Congress. Nic proudly shows the LBJ pen. There was another Greek boy before, but he ran off with a Chinese girl. I go back and sit on my wobbly wooden steps and look at the cherry trees in the yard. The butterfly helmets are flying around.

I am up next day to meet Clay Putnam, the coordinator of Creative Writing, who invites me to lunch in the faculty cafeteria. When we take our trays to the cashier, I am shocked—he does not pay. The U.S. is run by the Dutch. Putnam says, "We've just had Denise Levertov. She's a Londoner. I'm comfortable with people from London." Prologue. What is the semester like: cars drawing to the door with destination Pacific Heights or wherever, the talk may be in Yiddish, Karl Shapiro and friends can blast at radio–immortal Ezra Pound. Or Shirley Kaufman says, "Moshe Dayan sat in that chair last week," as her older husband adds, "I was a student of Dr. Freud. Do you know what he said to us students in Vienna one morning? 'People are divided into two groups, those who had books in their houses in their childhood, and those who had not.'" It seems a prologue to the new flower children of the world; flowers with lesson plans.

Mark Linenthal, the director of the Poetry Center, a new friend. He and his wife Frances see a psychiatrist first thing in the morning. Mark boasts he spends more than his professor's salary on the sessions. Wednesday afternoon, after the Center's reading, there shines the dream of unlimited booze; professors do not stock fridges with beer. The poets come marching through, in a few diamond months I get to know the bards of the 60's. Jim Wright is the Irish-style maestro, a Montague depth-charged; Wright is bard personified in his reciting and singing. He recites from memory for me Pearse and MacDonagh, the lords of the 1916 rising. Ed Field got his audience rocking with laughter at his reading (during which I take my private Nobel Prize out of my pocket and hand it to him); Jim

Chapson, who comes into my office because I sit on his Master's Committee, catches my eye and we start laughing.

At his reading George Stanley becomes a friend. A slight, rather clerical figure puts a statement on the chairs in the room. I pick it up and find it impressive. "I was born in San Francisco, January 7, 1934. So far, my education has been to read, write, and rationalise at St. Ignatius High School and U.C. Berkeley, and to gradually and painfully learn, at least once in a while, to stop rationalising and answer life more directly. This through further reading, conversations with Jack Spicer, and Louis Zukofsky. I love San Francisco and feel responsible for her. In addition to poet I accept the following identifications: homosexual, Catholic, and radical. Robert Duncan leads the clapping at the end of each poem. After it is over, two young men patiently wait to talk to George, they tell me they are from Milwaukee. George sees them and says to Frances, "Invite them." Frances, "Those girls over there?" "No, Frances, the boys." But I don't remember Antler and Jeff at the party.

The other track is Thursday to Tuesday. Kubly tells me the area at the top of the street is known as "The Swish Alps." Beyond them is Buena Vista Park, not quite as remarkable in song and story as Golden Gate, but still. Kubly takes me on a drive up there. On the summit a line of men are walking in a circle, concentrating in dead silence. Two break away and I watch a car speeding down the twists and turns of the descent. Is it a movie scene I've watched?

Sunday, Kubly looks in at noon, back from an Episcopal Mass. A student from Kentucky, David Polk, comes with his wife for advice on a book of poems. Mary Conlin turns up; all of this is Sabbath day gin drinking! To end the cycle, Kubly, a young faculty member called Brogan, and I, hit the Haight Street bars. We start in the Studio where the girls pack pistols to keep off the men. I must mention Mary Conlin and I dashed out in the afternoon for a stroll in Golden Gate: the bushes were moving with what seemed love, Buddhist monks danced and clashed their cymbals, the Phoenix Park is a poor cousin.

Beaches are only a short distance away. I have discovered the "J" car that goes out beyond the University of California hospital to a stretch of sand with debris, some wood, shy short waves on a pier. A bar is open right on the edge of the sandhills; large murals of the city's history decorate its walls, a contribution of the W.P.A. Workmen-mermen-barmen not far from the water's edge. I am told this beach became the paradise for the most convincing because the most conversational of poets, a paradise with a transistor held to his ear. Baseball scores had a background of waves for Jack Spicer. He was also the most controversial of poets. Another landscape was lying in Golden Gate Park, a radio swinging from a tree above his head.

In one of my writing classes there are a number of Black Panthers headed by a minister in their government, George Murray. They bring armed bodyguards and the College wants to know if I want cops in the classroom. Most of their writing efforts involve the word "Honky." I compare their effusions to Irish rebel poems. The campus slowly explodes in endless faculty debate, specially the R.O.T.C. controversy. I find it impossible to vote with conservatives, but part of me is inclined to harken to the cautious (nonforgotten wise words) of Clay Putnam against banning it. Politics looks worse on television, I note as I see the campus rallies on Kubly's set.

Tallyrand is the greatest sugar daddy, life just before the revolution is sweet. Ron drifts through in mail uniform, upsets his wife by not returning home at night. David is younger, we quiver in our chairs when we talk about poetry. Then we quiver like Venus's arrows, he makes a terrible face and blackeyes me. Stars do a Salomé dance. He arrives next afternoon and tells me he is getting married in February. Jim is a mystic (and a Cromwellian like me). He is so intense he can not talk much. He sits in my office with his folder of poems, waiting for a new universe. Revolution and inclination mean classes in students' houses and specially in my basement; alcohol permitted during course period, no marijuana until it is over. At Hallowe'en we stay on till 4 a.m., blasted and participants in a delicious reading of Williams's "Asphodel, That Greeny Flower" in some kitchen. Spicer's "Billy The Kid" a wilder and wilier poem follows.

I call the apartment Grail Castle or the Spaceship, one is flying over the Bay, one over the cosmos. After the Cavafy reading for Greek Independence Day I invite everyone back to the Spaceship. Only Jameson Ten is served. Duncan appreciates this but leaves early. George and Jim become friendly and double up in laughter; some souls imbibe whiskey for the first time, and it is still daylight. My student Frank totals his car as he drives away and has to get stitches in his face. At the party he tells me he is a Norbertine priest from Green Bay, Wisconsin, gay, and wishes to make me a mouth-watering vegetarian dinner (later he invites me to Mass in some suburb, and substitutes my name for Jesus Christ in the Canon, I flee out the door). I persist in going out with the group left; we hie to The Pioneer (not the same meaning in both cultures) on Van Ness presided over by Enda Bartley, from Ballyjamesduff. He gives me the address of a man he says I'd like, George Gleeson, ex-member of Limerick County Council, who "wore the Blue Shirt." The Irish Consul sits on the jukebox and buys us a drink, his toast "To the local maidens and lads."

What are we but pub tribes? Harrington's, McCarthy's on Market Street, The Jug of Punch on Mission Street (music on Sundays), The Abbey on Geary Boulevard (music on Saturdays), and back home Terry's on Haight Street: full of cops after Paddy Wagon trips snaring hippies. Some nights I can sneak underage students in and the cops are friendly. The bartenders are from Dingle and have the G.A.A. scores. Sundays the hippies block the street in early evening, cops on horseback intervene. The people's Sabbath protest against Capitalist traffic is led by one Charlie Manson who also came to my reading at the I-Thou café.

Campus talk, President Summerskill has resigned from a pay phone at the airport, the Black student newspaper has been raided. The Panthers in my class have disappeared. Barbed wire appears around the campus; politics seems a class of earthquake that spills at intervals over talkative hermetic cells. I tell Nic the story of our colleague, Bill Dickey the poet, who murmurs beside me on the street car going home, "Do you know what my favourite century is, the 18th century."

Tom Hill drives me and Jim out past the Golden Gate Bridge, over steep twisty roads, to Stinson Beach. The beach spreads its arms like my home sand of Kilkee. Spicer and Duncan used to deckchair here; the first drank, the second never rested (Duncan typed Billy the Kid). Tom's photographer friend dances around in purple pants; after his camera stops swinging in the wind we recite a little Spicer:

> Its beaches we've starved on. Or loved on...
> It roars at me like
> love. And
> Its sands wet with the new tide.
> Automatic
> Only, for Christ's sake, surf.

I step into the cave of the White Rabbit. This rabbit is never what you expect, there have been many resplendent and fragmentary disguises: here a droll Scotsman californiaed into verse's turf and surf; Graham Mackintosh, hero of West Coast chronicles of poetry, White Rabbit publisher; later Black Sparrow printer, co-maker of Spicer's books. He presides over a giant Natoma Street print den where cushions are strewn on the floor; men drink, women smoke dope. There are children around, I am afraid of sitting on one.

Graham is bringing out John Allen Ryan's second book. John is a major ex of Ginsberg's, though he refuses to talk about him. John, erstwhile bartender at The Place, keeps the most comprehensive literary journal, in five sections across the page. He is deadly leaving a pub, after we leave Gino's and Carlo's he propositions each young man on the street, yelling like a siren. I wander off a bit, some of these guys look dangerous. John's proudest bar boast is "My eight Irish great grandparents were all Protestants." How can I drink to that?

Richard Brautigan is a silent presence on Natoma Street, tall and spiry; he is part of Graham's lark. White Rabbit has brought out his *Please Plant This Book*, seed packets in a folder: squash, parsley, lettuce, carrots, others, and native California flowers. The announcement says, "This book is free, permission is granted to reprint this book by anyone as long as it is not sold." The project carries the twist of the publisher's mind, a menu of fine printing, surrealism, Celtic capriciousness. Brautigan is beginning to sell, he's just out in German; he collects WWII machine guns and rifles.

Jim, Graham, and I often retreat to the bar on the corner of Natoma and Howard where Graham can make his disquisitions, "State is nothing, it all happens at Cal. You get independent opinion there. Do you know the poet and the poem Spicer liked best in the language? Edward Lear; the greatest poem was 'The Jumblies.'" The phone on the wall starts ringing, I do the McDaid's thing and answer. The blacksweatered barman yells, "Drop it, faggot, can't you mind your own fucking business, keep your nose clean or you'll be out of here." I suggest withdrawal and we arrive in Gino and Carlo's, green walls, pool table in back, the best literary graffiti I've seen, and on the stools Charles McCabe *San Francisco Chronicle* columnist, beside Pierre Salinger's ex-wife. The jukebox that Spicer pushed cut-up matchboxes into to shut off the Beatles. I get the impression glasses may fly at any moment.

Back at the campus, we are having a community of poets reading for Marin County high school kids at the Poetry Center. We poets sit in a circle, I am beside Jo Miles in a wheel chair, George Stanley on my other side. As Linenthal introduces the occasion, Black militants filter in; Linenthal explains these kids have come a long way to hear poetry. The intruders whistle eerily, their leader plays with the microphone, "The campus is closed." I wonder how George and I are going to manage Jo Miles. Brautigan gets up and says, "These guys have a cause, let's allow them to do what they want to do, we should agree with their wishes and leave." About half the circle gets up and leaves, including Duncan. George stays, and Jo is still beside me when we see the National Guard in the back of the gallery. We proceed with our reading, maybe a poet among the kids will remember this day.

Graham starts talking about a book; he wants me to edit an anthology of Californian poetry. I write to a crowd, including Bukowski who writes back and sends me signed copies of two books (the only poet to refuse is Richard Duerden). Some are chagrined at this move; James Schevill my colleague refers with horror to Spicer's hornet letters stored at the Center. He and his friends call the Spicer/Duncan group "The North Beach Hominterm." I am interrupted by graver news, a telegram from my sister tells me Kavanagh is dead. I phone Tony Cronin in Missoula and send a telegram and letter to Katherine Kavanagh. Paddy makes *The San Francisco Chronicle*, "For 30 years Kavanagh held court on the Irish literary scene, usually from a bar stool." My captain is dead though I am among the captains and the kings.

Kubly begins talking about another writer I hold close who has died, Carson McCullers, who visited Galway just before I left. Endearing photos of her and John Huston at her bedside were in the press. Death takes angel–writers to heaven. "When I was at Yaddo I came down to breakfast and as I crossed the yard to the dining room I heard a wailing like a dog confined somewhere; the fountain in the yard contained a bundled–up McCullers who shortly was packed off into an ambulance."

Kubly takes me to dinner to a wealthy friend with a Swedish writer-wife. George Hornstein begins with de Valera and stays on Israel. George is a produce king and he says California will not be growing vegetables in 20 years. He presents us with a gold bottle opener and a penknife for cutting whiskey tops. There is an aside—I mention that Dan Reeves the owner of the Los Angeles Rams is my mother's first cousin. George knows him well and grins, "He doesn't remind me of you at all, he doesn't like poetry. Dan Reeves only likes horses and women."

The world began with a book, Genesis, Gilgamesh; this world ends with one. Graham takes an interest in a triptych of poems Tom Hill, Jim and I put together. We call it *Blue House* after a phrase of Tu Fu; drifters in houses of merriment though what we really mean is the golden shifting foreign haze we live in, that delights us. Ron Mackintosh takes photos of us as we lean against the Natoma wall with cans of Miller in our hands (pointing to the future?). Graham prints an invitation: a proclamation on dark blue paper of wining and dining in a Blue House, 574 Natoma Street, with the injunctions, "Wear your masks, bean curd will be served (soft and hard). (No poems will be served). No poets will be served."

Of course poems keep on being served.

New Orleans: The Quarter

Vessels sailing further up the river never carry a cargo of flowers. Flowers stop here.

Site of pushing the forward instincts to the limit.

What I wish is insurgency. That can be said with flowers. The seemingly mild flags, the purple, the white, are the morning's soldiers. They die first. They give up their petals for the future—reincarnation.

The light from the earth in a city.

Under the sun of the new world you march to a different waterfall. Spouted Cupids and Venuses engage in swimming. O Bella Roma built on new swamps. Carnival built on slavery. Canal digging by the Irish who were worth nothing.

The Morning Glories just down the street from the door are all over the parking lot, on the side of the slave quarters (now apartments), in profusion along the walls. When you get up late morning is still with these blooms, a parade ground of paradise. In the street the dingy, the seedy, the infected, the going shortly to heaven. Then we go to Buster Holmes's 35 cents plates of beans and rice.

We must remember how our blossoms came when we were young. We were thick as leaves and desperate; freaks, souls. We thought we would not see the end of the Vale of Despondency after the next outburst of Irish rain.

The smell of olive trees now in Jackson Square, not decay, but ruin.

This is where the city comes from. Dig, flood, dig. River bank to cathedral. After Mass handshake in the Square, the Archbishop's hand is that of a butcher's son from Tipperary town.

The smell in the air among the canvasses the artists in shorts hang on the park railings beside Mississippi jockeys with horses and carriages.

The French fleet is in, the Archbishop speaks to them in bad French on NATO. Wolfwhistle ghosts.

Degas painted here; a room of his paintings in City Park. Cotton Exchange; alligators in the bayou, paddle boats, a bar.

Sweetest, tiniest, caged zoo. Audubon Park, Robert Stone's exhaling arena.

Trumpet vines. A new curtain for the alcoholic tribes mowing the streets with their high colour and mottled hands. Fairies, fingers round the glass. The image of the young Keats serenades. He would get attention here, though we are far from the Spanish steps (yet walking closely to them). There exists that dimension: death, inherited from Spain and France. St. Louis a capricious bride in river dying, the fever of crusades.

Go back then to the garden beds of the Quarter.

Temple manias of the sun, spinning courtyards, rayholes, masonry stems, tendrils over cobblestones. I bend an ivy shoot to point it backwards to the wall it is intended to train on. Ivory cameos, seized roses, wisteria.

A watering can is never here for effect. You can't get real owls into the Quarter anymore—but to hell with plastic owls.

The Context of The Quarter

"1000 block St. Ann. James Liddy, 39, told police he was walking towards the river on St. Ann about 11 p.m. when he was accosted by a man and two women who threatened him with a revolver and robbed him of $15 in currency, $60 in traveller's checks and a passport." The *States-Item*, May 30, 1975.

As usual they got it wrong, I was coming from Ireland via Bowling Green, Ohio, where I was interviewed for a job that morning. Arriving from the New Orleans airport, I was wearing a suit. The currency amounts were much larger, the muggers were one man and two drag queens. I was walking at St. Ann and Burgundy towards the side bar door of the Burgundy Inn where Jim and Hank were waiting for me. As a result, I was stateless without ID hanging around the Immigration office on Canal Street, they didn't believe I was a citizen.

New Orleans is very beautiful, I'm living in the French Quarter where the architecture is Spanish. Cheap, cheap. Draft beer for 35 cents and spirits for 50 cents There are quite a few street musicians, a five piece jazz band, complete with full set of drums, is playing in the middle of Royal Street. There is a television camera across the street and I see a pool of blood on the sidewall; I ask one of the people standing around what is happening and he says Oh they had a geek show; a "geek" is someone who bites the head off a live chicken. Two geeks and two chickens performed, luckily I missed it.

The apartment is lovely, a whole third floor on Conti overlooking a courtyard of banana trees. $135 a month, opposite the wax museum. From the landing you can see the steeple of the St. Louis mortuary chapel. The windows overlook high buildings on Canal Street. Bourbon Street is two blocks away, up a bit the pink balcony of Arnaud's restaurant. In the street I hear a man who looks like Luke Kelly singing, "Three lovely queens in a teashop/each in a marvellous dress."

"Ernest Larson, 19, of 2129 19th St., was turned over to New Orleans police yesterday after his arrest. He was booked with the murder of James Henry Roberson III, 37. The killing occurred shortly after midnight at the corner of Conti and Burgundy. Earlier yesterday New Orleans police arrested 19 year old Lori A. Yates, 7715 Trapier St. and booked her with the same offense. The victim was stabbed in the heart, face, chest and arms. The woman's companion took a butcher knife from the woman's purse and began stabbing Roberson. The man and woman fled, leaving the victim behind lying on the street with a knife protruding from his right eye. Police said the victim was not acquainted with the man and woman." The *States-Item*, 16 September, 1975.

I am in The Little Clubhouse around the corner where I see figures running by outside. Hank at home was sitting by the window and heard the shouting, he couldn't see the action as he couldn't find his glasses.

The bars open for twenty-four hours, some have no locks on their doors (a problem at Hurricane time), three eight hour shifts.

The Program of the Quarter

Jim and Hank go to Johnny Matassa's where you can have sex in the bathrooms, smoke dope outside the door on St. Philip, meet English teachers from Delgado Community College. Springsteen's favourite bar. It seems a real castle except for "knight" read "freak." A great Southern lady may be presiding, Miss Ivy, who loves Jim and gives him free drinks. "People are no damned good, Jim," Ms. Ivy intones. The other bartenders are Tiny, a drug dealer, Micky, Don, and Louis the founder's grandson who hates it and lurks in the grocery. Micky says, "Miss Ivy and I are the greatest friends in the world," and when Ivy's shift comes she says, "I can't stand that bitch, Micky." Miss Ivy arrives to stock, the coolers are stuffed with marijuana, "Tiny has left no goddamn place to put the beer." Don is a Scotsman who tells you the amount in his bank accounts; he's a friend of Jim and Hank. He goes from behind the bar to do "the bump" when the jukebox is right. His boyfriend Jan leaves him dinner on the counter.

The Sipos family are the kings of the bar, scions of a great Quarter dynasty, the Earlys of Royal Street. The three sons appear here before and after the racetrack. They are great macho boys; their mother Patsy adores Gumbo and conversation, she manages the Pontalba building for the city (the oldest apartments in the country). Then there are the architects Patrick Gondolfo and Walter Ernst, the quiet Scylla and the loud Charybdis. The waves gnash for hours which does not interfere with airports rising or public building getting new roofs.

Gondolfo had an armed fortress on Rampart Street. He had gotten the one disease one can't have in the Quarter:

fear of the streets. He was told he had a heart condition. Donald advised him on bypass procedures, but instead he went home and shot himself. Walter was the loudest customer in the bar, but that didn't prevent presenting Denver airport to us skypeople. When he died he was waked in the refurbished Mint. He was a connoisseur of Jaguars and finally was able to afford an old one; it was parked in the Mint compound with his ashes in the driver's seat. Everyone got so drunk they forgot about the car until the next day. The mourners had trouble getting back through security to rescue Walter.

SHOE TIME FOR MATASSA'S

Eva is just out of jail and comes up to me. "Do you want to fuck me." "No." "Why not?" "I just want to talk." "You can talk to me, honey." "I want to talk to someone over there." "You mean you want to talk to that man." She goes off in disgust. Later she dances to the jukebox, but business is bad.

The Quarter is sad, the plane went down, teeming rain. The calls keep coming to the bars, so and so is dead. In Matassa's an old queer weeps, "That's a prick I'll never see again." I am sitting with Jim and Miss Russell, a most amiable drag queen (on certain days). I have just bought her a drink at her request and I have noted that the Episcopal Bishop of Louisiana was aboard, "I see lightning has struck the Protestant Bishop." Russell: "Fuck her." Later Russell: "Fuck The Pope, she's a bitch." "Russell, will you fuck off to Belfast."

Next morning, on cure, I pass the open door of Brennan's restaurant; waiters weeping at the counter, their head waiter is dead.

Bars are eternal, life changes. The Playhouse is on Dauphine, ten minutes nearer than Matassa's, just over from the pink cottage where *A Street Car Named Desire* was typed into the light of the world (the street car used to go down Bourbon Street, now you see the Desire bus in the distance).

The cast of characters is also desirable and beautiful here.

Verbal Wren "Jane" who walked on bare feet from Oklahoma in the forties because she heard there was good servicemen business in the Quarter. She made enough to start the bar and now lives next to Mrs. Boggs, the Congresswoman. Bobby Hand, the kindest Celtic bartender in the world, whose brothers are cops, pours free drinks to the brim after midnight when Jane leaves. Miss Kitty who is small and from the Midwest—kind too. One half of the bar is white, there's lots of oilrig workers from the Gulf. The other half is the back, drag queens training young black males in crossdressing. They practice in the bathroom.

A working class bar. The chiropractor from next door between patients, Irish-American Jimmy Maloney with bayou fables. Fay, with pure heart, who is as proud of being an octoroon as knowing her Catechism. We talk about who made the world. She is so generous, after she comes back from seeing the Tulane boys in cabs she buys drinks for the house. She is a saint.

A warrior selling "An Poblacht" wins out on Saturday night. The Cajun waiters come around 4 a.m. when the restaurants are cleaned and closed; beer listening to extraordinary patois. Daylight, the streets are hosed down, the vendors begin to set up.

I meet someone who was educated in a Benedictine monastery in Arkansas. We talk about St. Benedict and his rule for so long that the laybrothers' cows come home about six a.m. Bobby tells us about Fr. Rogers, the police chaplain, who has been trapped a few times in the line of fire, Quarter hero.

(We hear Fr. Rogers's Mass in the St. Louis chapel later: he talks about his ancestral county Louth, same as Bobby's; quotes a Tom Moore song, invites us to Irish? coffee. Later too the furore over the Archbishop banning Masses in bars on St. Patrick's Day. No one gives a damn about paedophilia, but banning bar-Masses is too much. Over this New Orleans is ready to leave the Church.)

A friend from Missouri visits. A student type I will get used to, he has never read the New Testament; intense rows, mini-passes, endless session, until my guest takes an unexpected walk to the Greyhound Bus station. His best line is, "I can only give you a bad kiss compared to the ones I give girls." A second best, "I am very attracted to Hank, he is very handsome, and he is straight like me."

Leaving the station, I meet a man who has just been released from Angola, the prison up river, "Why even the chili in the Greyhound Bus station tastes good."

Over Labor Gay weekend the gay bars have free lunches and dinners. In Café Lafitte's in Exile we have screw-drivers and go up on the balcony with the paper plates. Two queens argue over how they will bring up their adopted son (or is it a fantasy one of them will become pregnant?) In the Bourbon Pub very early Michael Jackson clones munch.

Kitty remarks in the little Club Playhouse, "After work it's nice to have a little fun." Jim is exhibiting a need for Saturday night fun I haven't seen before. MacFaustus phones from Sao Paulo and introduces me to Rudi, announcing their nuptials. He says the bars are holes in the wall, puts all sorts of queens on the phone. He invites me to his wedding. I say I will go if they invite Adolph Hitler.

On the Playhouse 3 a.m. radio, I hear, "Kevin O'Kelly, NBC News, Dublin." Bobby tells me, "President de Valera is dead." Don, on safari from Matassa's, is beside me, "I thought that fucking bitch was dead years ago."

In the Dolpen bookstore on Royal Street an Italian says to the clerks, "You have copies of *The Purgatorio* and *The Paradiso* but none of *The Inferno*." The clerk says, "Only The Inferno seems to sell."

We go hungover into the Super Dome which has just opened. There are seats left only at the top. A Pontifical occasion; we see specks below at an altar, one of them is that "charismatic windbag" Fulton Sheen. Birds are flying around—a moment of terror, we think we are falling down on him. The big T.V. camera opposite switches on, Montini's sad face speaks from Rome, "We address you under the Dome of Heaven."

Introduction to Wisconsin

I was brought up in a great literary country, less than the size of Wisconsin with a smaller population and an equal number of taverns, that has produced—can I say—innumerable fiction writers and poets as well as four Nobel prize winners. I was blessed with literary memory when I began reading, something I see as partially absent from my students' days and nights. The best of them make up this deficiency; Wisconsin can shine with writers. Some souls are touched with a muse-wand in my UWM workshops. The teacher's function is to shove and embellish the musepower's golden proposals and to expand the memory of tradition. After arriving 25 years ago, I perceived Wisconsin too as a field full of writing folk. When I meet them I lift my champagne glass lakewards

A great awakening in Wisconsin has been Lorine Niedecker and Black Hawk island. This locus of genius has brought me again to the sense of the druid religion: sacred place. By her river she reminds me of Yeats in his tower at Ballylee on a stream. Lonely and Zukofsky-spurned, her "Paean to Place" is probably more considerable than "The Wild Swans at Coole." A great poet in your own country is the marker of tradition.

Milwaukee is a city of several poets, the first is the very beautiful personal lyricist Horace Gregory. One of the immortal backroom presences in American literature as an editor. I can dwell in a city described by him as "Gather, foregather/in the pale mist of Juneau's city:/Below it flows the thin Menomenee/Where forests were: clay-banked the silver river,/The trail in memory across the plain./ ...And from grey roots, the lilac flowering/In tombs that open when remembered spring/Comes home again beneath a tall roof-tree." Milwaukee somehow holds ancestral seeds; Gregory's grandfather, first city engineer, graduated in Dublin and claimed Lady Gregory as cousin. A faint air of Coole blows in Lake Park, the German socialists were landlords here so there should be more swans, and if not this plumage then more boats and lovers. People can concentrate around, sail on lakes and rivers.

Just this semester a young poet in my class Zack Pieper handed me some lines that reignite his home town, Mayville, "Forgive me, I am singing myself to sleep/bathtubs and saints, all planted upsidedown in the backyard/Blessed is the name of the forgetful,/those thoughtful old men with long walks to take./Those children who can never hurry home/ ...they are kissing the traintracks they are singing in their sleep."

"By an inland ocean," let us keep singing on the deck in the bad days, the good days, the long nights, the first window blue, first thirst.

No temporary spray of hymns.

Milwaukee Diaspora

God shift all here!

Not to be self-important or anything, but I am not a
nomad though I have been seized since adolescence with a
longing to live somewhere else, in a city of poets and
young men, a city with a history like Cavafy's and cafes
like Saba's. When I was young, I wished it to be a Spanish
speaking place; parks and railway stations open all night. I
practised the art of invisibility in Madrid, Valladolid,
Cordoba, Santiago de Compostela, Zamora. I became an
emigrant, an exile, a disappearing act, and an object on the
horizon in 1967 when I abandoned Dublin. I came out of
a literary and alcoholic culture at its most swan-songish and
worked in a succession of North American cities—San
Francisco, Portland, New Orleans, and Milwaukee. The
first of these drank as much as Dublin and had as many
loud and strong poets but not the same quality of bars
except for North Beach, while Milwaukee suggests Dublin
without the same quantity of poets but with the bars. New
Orleans was the giant tropical metropolis which it gleamed
so warm and sensual I could not see the poets, but the
jam-packed bars went twenty-four hours and so did I.

I have been in Wisconsin since 1976 and sometimes on
rainy days my new city reminds me of my old, though not
as much as The Loop in Chicago which holds Irish faces
in the downpour. Milwaukee can strike me as being as
stodgy and melancholy as Grafton Street in 1955; it is not
as stodgy as the provincial German or Polish city from
whose ashes it arises. But Grafton Street was never, not
even now, as American and erotic as Milwaukee's East
Side; an artificial paradise of desire, a little Berlin of the
twenties at least in the head. Close is some hours later;
and as I stand in the music of the last call I am the same

writer I would have been in Dublin yet I get the impression my stance is more energetic, concentrated on body and soul.

I am an exile, I am not an exile. "Exile" has enough alienation in it to be a real condition, yet it can be read as part of the flashy itinerant supernaturalism of the voyageur. The spirit wandereth whence it is employed or patroned. The artist type is outside the first social force of Mammy and friends; distance beckons new interruptions, and maybe memory spins into backlash.

Writing can seem the activity of alcoholic and workaholic ghosts; the famous never-tired ones: Wilde, Auden, Isherwood, used new domicile and flirtatious café in a more exuberant mode than they would at home. Do not dismiss the soldiering in far foreign fields where the battle cry is: do not tire.

The books on the table are piled-up differently: if I had stayed would my life have been changed by John Wieners, Lorine Niedecker, and above all Jack Spicer? Sitting by a great lake stung by the idea: your Ireland is dead, clarify your mind.

We swam like high-powered fish out of Modernism and we needed the ambivalences of travel. Fragmentation and change are stamped on our passports. Travel through loose twilight zones. Do I ever rework the Joycean formula: did I ever leave? Can one ever leave the pre-Vatican II church? You can see the spire from your window. Montague's quote, in my gilded McDaid's youth, out of Cavafy which moved me so much: you age in the same city, your hair eventually whitens in the same street. Images of the past, crowded dream, returns.

Yet there is no substitute for being in a new country with a clear mind, and friends from a different tribe. New starlets.

O prodigal, the home place is closed!

The Midwest, Remembering Nick Kubly

Nic Kubly was my first American friend. He was that now somewhat unrecognisable type: the heartland seigneur the Mid-western patrician. He was Swiss-American; his land, his New Glarus house, were habitations of a dual public trust. He conducted the Wilhelm Tell Orchestra personally.

Like those of us who survive into newer ages he became, malgre lui, a museum keeper. The symbol of his Arcadia was his '38 Buick, whose beautiful white tyres once ruled the earth. I have written elsewhere how my father and mother brought a '39 Buick back from New York via Southampton; those white tyres shone briefly on a medley of Irish roads. An early summer in the 70's we were in New Glarus for a Swiss frolic; all day on the Wisconsin farm. Some of Kubly's house guests worked on the old Buick which had been kept in a shed for the winter. Slowly it was brought back to perfect working order and fed its gasoline. We filed in and, with Nic at the wheel, we drove the mile to New Glarus: a faintly tourist town, we were serenaded by yodelling. A younger Wilhelm Tell popped up inside the bar.

I learnt that every few years New Glarus has gone to Glarus in Switzerland, one of the central meadows of Europe. Nic Kubly wrote the books they read on the plane.

Kubly was a traveller whose journals were part of his auto-biography. He combined in his best writing, place, fact, elaboration, and absolute timing. He had an equal sense of adventure and evasion about his life. He was the good American of the 40's/50's who ran into trouble in Wisconsin, to wit Joe McCarthy. The Irish boy was sure the Swiss boy was a fellow traveller! I think his best books were fuelled by protest against that alcoholic hysteria and by the desire to escape from home shores. The steady elegance of his views on democratic citizenship! The two works I like best are *An American in Italy* and *Easter in Sicily*. The former won the National Book Award when there were very few categories.

Love it and leave it and write about it.

I had good times with Nic in the heartland—it was he who brought me hence—parties in Racine, my first visits to Milwaukee (he was the grand restaurant reviewer for *The Milwaukee Journal*), gin and bucolic weekends on the farm. What stands out in my delayed memory? His friendship with Comparative Literature colleague Orph Johnson who learnt his first French as a G.I. liberating villages; the people ran to the well where they had hidden their wine to offer it to the Americans. Or the magic moment in the upstairs workroom of the farm when he displayed for me his erotic correspondence with Carl Van Vechten. What was in the other drawers? Once everyone was queer, now the post-Kinsey return to normality! No recollection hits me as much as my encounter with him in San Francisco, on my second day in the daisy new world.

This happens on the San Francisco State Campus. There is a man brooding over one of the desks: heavy glasses, white and grey sweater, a pile of manuscripts. He turns to tell me the guy in my place last semester committed suicide. I bless myself against the evil eye of California. A booming voice introduces, "I'm Nic Kubly, you're from Ireland, I was raised in New Glarus which is almost in Europe." He invites me for cocktails to his house on Waller Street. By the time I arrive from my downtown hotel, he has already talked to the landlord next door. There is a condemned basement I can have. Glasses in sturdy hands we go over to the English-born owner who lives over the basement. I hear the word "limey" for the first time. I whoopee into the night because I have landed at last.

The Haight-Ashbury! With Nic through the nearby Golden Gate Park, a massive scene, hippie flowers and love. The bushes shake with sex, magic substances. We wander to the museum, a magnificent Oriental collection. I pause at drawings by Jean Cocteau; there is a sexy one of Spender called "Stephen." I remember Paddy Kavanagh telling me how Spender had camped up his poems in the Encounter office, "violently beautiful." We drink jasmine tea in the garden. Nic tells me he is finishing up his Greek book. On the basis of my reputation as a monarchist I am to be given some chapters to look over (all the time he is concealing his friendship with Queen Frederika from me). So I have to examine the Corfu accounts of the Empress Elizabeth; the rage of beauty over grey hairs before the assassin's rage approaches the lakeboat at Lausanne. The madness of Bavaria, the calm of the Hapsburgs, as we watch the daily neo-revolution at San Francisco State. I can't quite grasp it, the campus has seemed to me a holy city with a pay check, the idea of the community a constellation of poets. Robert Duncan presiding over the chicken and pasta with Mark Linenthal, and me in the cafeteria. Politics, on the other hand, defines itself as a class of earthquake that spills at intervals over the hermetic assembly of cells we name the university. Nic is taking care of these "after shocks" we gaze at on television; we are happy-houred.

Nic wanders in at night into my cave after being on the town or at the party, I pour a drink he pours a story. The photograph in Spender's coffee table book on Auden: the not quite so young Senator John F. Kennedy presents the National Book Awards to W.H. Auden, John O'Hara, and

Nic! A pre-Camelot still. "The day after the ceremony, I was cruising on that section of the New York subway where you pick up guys. I saw Auden, and since I had spoken to him the day before, I greeted him. He snubbed me."

I remember that dinner party among the silverware of Pacific Heights where Nic fell asleep and woke up not aware of Republican glitterati company. He enumerated the New York bathhouse names in the 40's, a zealous kid's list from Madison, "I got to know Leonard Bernstein, Marlon Brando, and Stephen Spender. Spender's cock was the biggest I had ever seen, it was thick as a coffee can." Gore Vidal's brilliant autobiography, *Palimpsest*, suggests that Bernstein and Brando were the common "names" bragged about in New York, but I prefer to believe there are experiences. I believe also on great days William Blake's proposition that experience is holy.

Nic had unusual crystal-gazing powers. He told me, "You know Thornton Wilder only had sex in trains in Germany." I worried about what Wilder did during 1939–45, but maybe unnecessarily. Nic beamed when I conveyed a major piece of graffiti I found in a bathroom of the UWM campus, "Oscar was wild, but Thornton was wilder."

I visit Nic in the Spring of 1996, after many moons, and I am just in time. I caught him on his last weekend at his farm on Kubly Road (his father had been a state senator for a long time in Madison). He was 81, he recognised me, asked about my sister, we reminisced about San Francisco, and we talked about Kay Boyle, his one time patron. As Baroness Frankenstein she had brought him to San Francisco State, but they fell out when he required separate living quarters. His mind is intermittent, he goes looking for his "other wife" when his actual wife pours us drinks. I wander to the workroom upstairs and pause in memory of the Van Vechten letters. I have brought two friends, Tomás Larscheid and Jerod Schroeder; we are sitting cozily with the drinks when he booms at them, "You're not Swiss." Wilhelm Tell is still operating. We look at his last published book on Switzerland; it has a chapter about him and me in Zurich that contains arresting untruths.

The coming together of coincidence and affinity. A restaurant critic that shut restaurants, a European traveller who hummed and polished local myths, a farm boy out of the Mid-west with moonlight in his eyes who got further than the Wisconsin crossroads.

Mel

There are two kinds of friends: the younger and older. Same age friendship is more baroque and useless than same sex love ever could be. The grace of an elder connection is not very visible in the United States. Moreover I did not feel at home with the faculty of any age when I started teaching. I was, and am, a stranger in my lakeside grove of academe where my peers lack the excessive social manners I was brought up with.

Mel Friedman was a soulmate of a colleague. He was interesting—now that is something in an English Department. I liked what he was a scholar about: the interior monologue, Djuna Barnes the idealiser of passion, the Bray and Foxrock Joyce and Beckett, Carson McCullers, icon of tenderness.

He knew, and did not like, Saul Bellow. He entertained John Montague in his Yale room, had a spat with Wallace Fowlie. Mallarmè was his preferred poet, Whitman the worst option.

He was a backroom man in university presses, he read manuscripts, he knew everyone.

But we both practiced an ancient obsession: conversation. Mel was by nature proficient in that art most necessary to institutions of learning: gossip. Academic folklore was reserved for that important hour, the luncheon table (besides he knew food, had lived in Lyons as a student: garlic a blind spot). Mel understood this delightful activity as that internal branch of study that surveyed human nature to illuminate the details of the human condition. Part of his hold on people was the underground and background information he supplied, he interrogated hundreds of people at the MLA.

His auditors relished the sallies into the impossible and ridiculous; the follies of deans and administrators. Sometimes the Dean would be at the next table in the restaurant, a light tap on the leg produced no effect.

Mel was undoubtedly wry on a number of topics, but a vigilant eye never ceased to be amused.

On his way back from lunch one day he stopped me and asked, "Do you think the Jews are less persecuted these days?" Apparently he and a friend, Woody Allen's brother, would be attacked by the Brooklyn Irish kids coming back from school. His one Irish trip had been when he was in the military; a short visit to Dublin. He liked a martini or two, liked parties in his own house, liked talking long distance in his office. He was friends with his graduate students and got them jobs.

His was a formidable consciousness, that of a post-WWII campus mandarin; that era has ended.

I belonged a little bit to that privilege, though I like beer drinking.

Nightlight, Milwaukee

At Murray and Park

Estragon:	Tree?
Vladimir:	Do you not remember the times we heard the birds named Romeo and Juliet singing here?
Estragon:	I'm tired. I have to think about moving from my apartment.
Vladimir:	Take a good look at the tree, you won't see it from your window.
	(They look at the tree. Pubs have closed.)

Estragon (*loaded*): I don't hear any birds singing.

Vladimir:	When you worry about your apartment the songs aren't there, the throats hidden in the branches. Now it's covered with leaves and the birds, what melodies.
Estragon:	Why do you drag me here to say good night? Leaves, and leaves can't make anything happen.
Vladimir:	Do you even remember how we used to talk under the tree?
Estragon:	Memory. It hurts.
Vladimir:	We used to look at each other and pretend we were 16th century page boys or page girls!
Estragon:	We blathered on and on.
Vladimir:	The moon between the branches got close to your eyes, didn't it?
Estragon:	You could be hanged for love, that's what I think!
Vladimir:	The poet died on a tree, maybe we could ... hang there.
Estragon:	I have to tell you. I have a girlfriend for a week, but I will remember.
Vladimir:	Love is dual—and doomed.
Estragon:	Endlessly, talk your head out to me.

Park and Murray

Closing time.
The bars are out,
looking down the street,
the nursing home.

I will love you
until the ambulance comes.